# OLTON HERITAGE

Jean Paine

Margaret Jordan

Carol Andrews

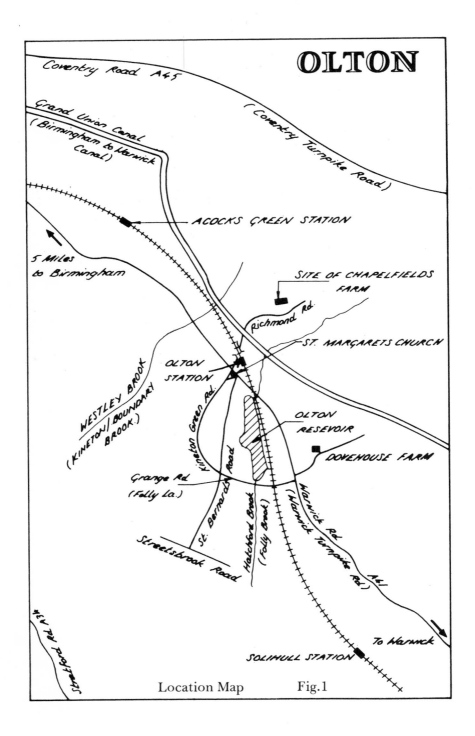

Location Map          Fig.1

# OLTON HERITAGE

by Jean Powrie

Margaret Jordan

Carol Andrews

First published September 1986 by
K.A.F. Brewin Books, Studley, Warwickshire.

© Jean Powrie 1986 — Exploring The Past
© Margaret Jordan 1986 — Victorian Heyday
© Carol Andrews 1986 — Changing Scenes and
Famous People

ISBN  0  947731  14  8  Paperback Edition
ISBN  0  947731  15  6  Hardback Edition

*Typeset in Baskerville and printed by
Supaprint (Redditch)Ltd., Redditch, Worcestershire.*

*Made and printed in Great Britain*

# CONTENTS

## ACKNOWLEDGEMENTS

The authors would like to thank the following:—

The Central Library, Birmingham. Birmingham Museum and Art Gallery, Solihull Central Library, Warwickshire County Records Office, Mrs. S. Bates Local History Department Solihull Library, Prof. F.W. Shotton MBE., FRS., Mr. C. Cattanach, Dr. William Powrie.

Miss Birthe Fox and Mrs. Betty Bancroft for help with typing, and those people too numerous to mention by name without whose help this book would not have been possible.

## ART WORK

The authors would like to express their appreciation to Sarah Jennings for providing the drawings for Olton Heritage.

# LIST OF PHOTOGRAPHS

# INTRODUCTION

This is believed to be the first ever history of Olton. It has been produced by three local residents and aims to give the area its own place in the story of Solihull of which it now forms a part.

Until the Victorian development this part of rural Warwickshire changed very little, most of what is now modern Olton formed the Lyndon Quarter of the parish of Bickenhill and was administered from distant Meriden. It was not until 1874 that Olton became part of Solihull for administrative purposes.

This three part history of Olton from earliest times to the 20th Century aims to reveal something of Olton's rich historical heritage.

# EXPLORING THE PAST

by Jean Powrie

1

# EXPLORING THE PAST

*CHAPTER 1: EARLIEST TIMES*

## Pre-history

The early story of our area can only be told in general terms, related to changes in climate, water distribution and soil content. Though apparently remote from recorded History, physical changes have affected the local Geography and, consequently, the habitation patterns and activities of those who reside, and resided, here.

That span of geological time known as the Pleistocene (most recent) period saw the Ice Ages, when glaciation was interspersed with warmer seasons.

## Lake Harrison

The second of the two glaciations which affected the area initiated dramatic physical changes. During this time there is evidence that two glaciers, advancing simultaneously from the North and down the Severn Valley, created a 50 mile long glacial lake. Professor Shotton has designated this lake 'Lake Harrison', after the Birmingham school-teacher who first noted its existence at the turn of the century.

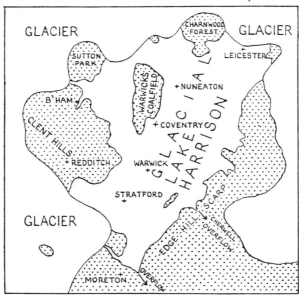

Fig. 2. The maximum extent of Lake Harrison impounded by ice-fronts and high land along the present-day valleys of the Avon, Soar and Tame. Unglaciated land, at this stage, is shown dotted. (Reproduced by kind permission of Professor Shotton and The Coventry and District Natural History & Scientific Society.)

2

## The Gilbertstone

As the ice melted, the water carved its way out and the River Avon was formed. The boulder clay, deposited by the glaciers, provided material for potters, tilers and, later, brick manufacturers. Rich keuper marl encouraged afforestation and agriculture. The glaciers also brought tougher rocks, foreign to the area and rounded by action. Several of these erratics[1] still survive in the Birmingham area. In our locality, one, known as the Gilbertstone, is remembered, together with Gilbertstone House from which it probably took its name, in Gilbertstone Avenue. Its history can be traced back at least to 1609.

An account of the perambulation of the Yardley parish bounds, made in that year, describes how, after crossing "Coventrye Way" and passing through the grounds of Gilbertstone House (owned in 1495 by Richard Acocke, but in 1609 by William Biddle), the lane, where "the stone called the Gilbertstone" lay, was reached. At this time the stone appears to have been used as a boundary marker.

In the 1937 residential development of the area, the stone was moved to a grass verge beside the Coventry Road. With changes in the road in 1952, it was transferred to Lyndon Green Junior School and, in 1978, to Blakesley Hall, Yardley, where it may still be seen beside the herb-garden. (Fig.1)

Plate 1          The Gilbertstone. Once used as a boundary marker.

Although the Gilbert Stone has seen several moves in recent times, legends stress past difficulties encountered by those attempting to move or lift the stone. It seems unlikely that it travelled far from the place where it was first deposited in the Pleistocene period.

## After Glaciation

As the last Ice Age passed, and Lake Harrison disappeared, trees re-covered the land. Continuing archaeological exploration suggests human habitation has always been more widespread and varied than hitherto believed, so it is not unlikely that humans returned to the area, to hunt and clear the forests and fish the waters of what was to become Olton.

## The Greek Connection

Several legends exist concerned with the early inhabitants of Britain. Geoffrey of Monmouth makes a colourful and romantic case for a hero, Brutus (thus Briton) leading an escaped band of Trojan slaves. This island might well have provided a secure refuge for such fugitives from Ancient Greece, for its remote geographical position placed it beyond the centres of civilized activity. Such Greek writings as survive suggest it was not until the fourth century B C. that the existence of the British Isles was recognised in the Mediterranean world.

In the time of Alexander the Great (356 – 323 B C), Pytheas claimed to have "travelled all over Britain on foot". His works, unfortunately, have only survived in second-hand fragments.

Trade usually follows the route of the explorer, and the westward commercial expansion of the Greeks, about 300 B C gives some support for Pytheas' claims. However, there is no firm archaeological evidence for any early Anglo-Greek connection. In England, B.C. Greek 'finds' are, not surprisingly, rare. Of the 200 or more early Greek coin discoveries so far recorded, one large group is known, and another is suspected, to have come from recent collections. Single coins are more promising, historically. Some have been discovered on known Iron-Age sites, suggesting that they have been in this country at least since the first century B C.

## The Olton Coin

Olton is not without a share in these finds, for an unusual and early Greek coin was discovered on the Olton-Acock's Green boundary. This coin has been identified as a genuine silver stater, struck in Messene during the fourth century B C.

Messene, a city on the slopes of Mount Ithome in the south-west Peleponnese, was established c369 B C as a bulwark against Sparta. It is appropriate that a coin of this city, which dominated the most fertile tract in Greece, should display the head of Demeter (goddess of the harvest) crowned with a wreath of corn. On the reverse side, the local (Ithomates) version of Zeus (King of the Gods) is depicted, striding, brandishing a thunderbolt and holding an eagle. The inscription reads

ΜΕΣΣΑΝΙΩ(N) (of the Messanians)

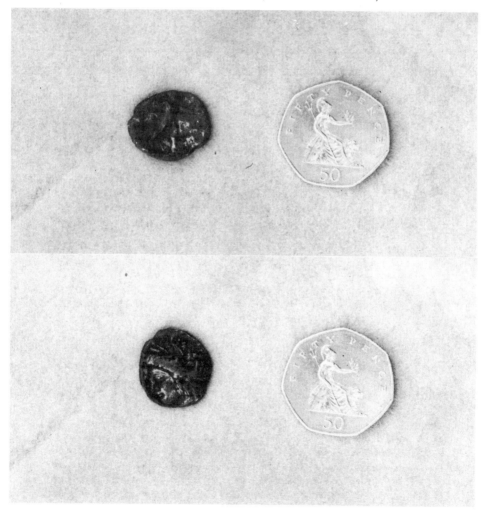

Plate 2     The Olton Coin — found on the Acocks Green/Olton border.

5

When a coin is found, all that is certain is that it arrived where it was discovered at a time after it was minted, but this does not prohibit speculation. This coin is old enough to have been brought here by Pytheas, or one of his followers. It is badly corroded, suggesting either a long, or chemically unfortunate, sojourn in the earth. It may have come through the tin trade, where coins must have been used much as we later used trinkets in our trade with less civilised peoples. Although Greek coins have been found near Hadrian's Wall and other Roman military outposts, it is difficult to imagine that a rare, and, even then, at least 350-year old, coin would be in the possession of an ordinary Roman soldier, although it might have graced the collection of some wealthy Roman Graecophile. That the coin came from a more recent, 18th or 19th century, collection, is a possibility which cannot be dismissed. There is no certain answer and, to this date, this coin's twenty-four centuries of history remain a tantalizing blank.

## Caesar's "People of the Interior"

In 55 B C Julius Caesar not only put Britain firmly on the map, but provided some information about its inhabitants. He identified "the people of the interior" as an older, less civilised race than the settlers of the South. Living on milk and meat and wearing skins, they appear as hunters and herders. Caesar's contemporary, Strabo, makes more general comments. His phrases "not skill enough to make cheese", "totally unacquainted with horticulture and matters of husbandry", "producing dogs sagacious in hunting", and "forests are their cities" could well be applied to these early Midlanders. Their nomadic, transitory way of life would explain why they left so little impression on the landscape.

## The Advent of Christianity

After the eventual conquest of Britain by the Romans, the lives of "the people of the interior" were affected by Christianity. It was well established before St Augustine brought the official romanised version in 597, and possibly arrived by several different routes — brought to Glastonbury by the "secret disciple", Joseph of Arimathea; sought from Pope Eleutherius by King Lucius; or advanced by soldiers and settlers from Rome. It is at a Roman fort, Manchester, that the earliest evidence of Christianity in England (c 185 AD) has been found.[2]

British Christians suffered persecution during the visit of the Emperor Severus (208 — 211 AD). Tradition names Christianfield, near Lichfield (Lich = corpse) as the site of a local massacre. Their descendants were driven into Wales by the pagan Saxons, who are reputed to have landed in 495 AD under Cerdic and "fought with the Welsh in the same day".

## The Hwicce

A long struggle between Saxons and Britons continued until 577 AD, recorded in the Anglo-Saxon Chronicles and lamented in Welsh poetry. The exhaustion of both sides opened the way for the Hwicce, the next people to have inhabited the area.

F M Stenton defines the Hwicce as "a people who, in the seventh century, occupied the territory now represented by Gloucestershire, Worcestershire and the western half of Warwickshire". They were almost certainly Angles, possibly originating from Schleswig. They penetrated the country at the Severn estuary, thrusting northward through the Severn and Avon valleys, bringing with them agricultural skills. They were already established in 603 AD when Bede describes the meeting between St Augustine and the Welsh Christians at an oak, "which lies on the border between the Hwicce and the West Saxons".

The area they occupied still bears a plethora of place names incorporating wic or wick (the Angle hard 'c') from Wicwar, near Bath, to Warwick. The settlement at Warwick, which had earlier been known by its Celtic name Guarth, was probably re-named under the Hwiccas. In the Burghal Hidage (B) of 918, it appears as Waeringwicum. Worcester is severally called Wic-wara-ceaster, or Civitas Wicciorum.

Although the Hwiccas succumbed to the Mercians from 716 – 796, first under Ethelbald and then under Offa, they retained some political and religious autonomy. Hwicce remained a separate see, with its Bishops at Worcester, and several leaders are shown taking independent action.

## The Lady of Mercia

In c.911,[3] a few years after the death of Alfred the Great, Mercia was ruled by Ethelfleda, widow of the Lord of Mercia and daughter of Alfred. With hostile Danes in the North and Welsh in the West, she and her army must have been constantly in the field. She established a parabola of forts, including one at Warwick. On her death (c 918), her daughter "was deprived of all authority and taken to Wessex".

## Vandalism — ancient and modern

In the troubled times which followed, the towns fortified by Ethelfleda offered some protection and so grew in importance. In contrast, the open countryside was harried to such an extent by internal strife and Nordic invaders, that the invaders themselves were forced to leave the country in order to find food and shelter. When Cnut penetrated Mercia (c 1013), his orders were "to ravage the open countryside, pillage the churches, burn the towns and put every male to the sword". "From Watling Street to the Thames", added Florence of Worcester, "these instructions were observed".

Plate 3          Bury Mound — an early earthwork at nearby Solihull Lodge.

Evidence of this Danish intrusion may be found in the nearby Solihull Lodge earthwork, now known as Bury Mound.(Plate 3) The Victoria County History for Warwickshire (1904) states: "a century ago it seems to have been called 'Dane's Camp' ", and identifies the mound with other pre-Christian earthworks. Surrounded by streams and marsh, this small hill would have offered security, a base, or a short-term residence to the invaders and to others.

Unfortunately, like so much of our heritage, this notable earthwork has suffered continually at the hands of man. The ramparts were substantially reduced between 1831 and 1872. A systematic excavation, necessary to illuminate the mound's origins and use, has yet to be undertaken.

*Mercia under Cnut*

Cnut's struggle for England, first against Ethelred II (popularly known as 'The Unready'), and secondly against Ethelred's son, Edmund Ironside, brought further destruction to our region. The Hwicce, under Eldorman Leofwine, came under attack from both Cnut and the treacherous Edric, Earl of Mercia.

During the conflict, Edric changed sides three times. He finished on the winning side and, in 1017 the Victorious Court confirmed his over-lordship of Mercia. Four years later, however, his treachery was remembered when he was cut down during the Christmas feast, in London. His Mercian estates were distributed amongst various Danish chiefs, but some of these, fearing the hostility of the inhabitants, sold the land and returned to Denmark.

The end of Cnut's reign saw the creation of three new Earls; Siward of Northumbria, Godwin of Essex and Leofric, son of the Hwiccan Leofwine and husband of the more famous Godiva, of Mercia.

## The Saxon Manors of Olton

Before Cnut's invasion, the two Saxon manors, Ulversleah and Cinctune, from which Olton developed, were firmly established. Both are mentioned in Saxon charters. Ulversleah in Worcestershire was, in 866, "given in exchange" to King Burgred of the Mercians (852 – 874). "Cinctunes broc" (Kineton Brook) is recorded as one of the bounds of Yardley Parish in 972.

## Ulversleah

The name, "Ulversleah", suggests that this settlement originated from a clearing made in the forest of Eardene, the Saxon form of Arden, by one called Ulver or Wolver (U and double U being interchangeable). Leah is the old English for clearing, still used in poetry as 'lea'. The 's', as today, denoted possession.

## Cinctune

Cinctune was at some time a cyningstun, or Royal manor, 'cyning' being the Saxon for 'one born of kings' and 'tune' meaning an estate. Such manors were centres for justice and taxation. Peasants from the surrounding countryside would bring their rents in food to the king's estates. Of necessity, there would be a manor house for the king's representative, huts for the workers, storage barns and a prison. (A law of Alfred states that "a man who has broken his pledge must go to prison for 40 days at the Cyningstun"). There would probably be a chapel, a bell-tower and a mill. A king's estate usually enjoyed tax concessions, but was required to support the king and his retinue, for a limited stay, when necessary.

The late Saxon period saw changes which must have affected Cinctune. With the expansion of trade, certain king's estates grew in importance, offering safety and commerce to travelling merchants, while others, alienated from the king's desmesne, were given to thegns in return for military support.   Certain thegns seized the opportunity to amass property, and the tenth century sees the emergence of substantial land-owners, with widely scattered estates.   Two such, Turchil of Warwick and Colswein of Lincoln, are shown as still owning this type of property in the survey of 1086.

*The Eve of 1066*

During the reign of Ethelred's surviving son, Edward the Confessor (1043 - 1066), Cnut's three Earls continued in power.   Harold Godwin (son) succeeded his father in 1053.   Siward's death in 1055, and the absence of a suitable heir (his eldest son having been killed in the previous year fighting for Malcolm of Scotland against Macbeth) sharpened the rivalry between the families of Leofric and Godwin.   The Godwins, over all, held the ascendancy.   Leofric's son, Elgar, was twice exiled, almost certainly at Harold Godwinson's instigation, and restored only with the military support of Griffin of Wales.

Elgar, who became Earl of Mercia by his father's death in 1057, himself died in 1062, leaving Mercia to his young and inexperienced son, Edwin.   The way was open for Harold Godwinson to gain the English Crown.

The dying Edward the Confessor, reputedly acknowleging the youth of the true heir, Edgar Atheling, and the troubles by which the country was beset, named Harold as his successor.   Wisely, the Lords of Mercia and Wessex resolved their differences and Harold married Edwin's sister, Edith.

## The Background to the 1086 Survey

After Harold Godwinson's defeat and death at the Battle of Hastings in 1066, William the Conqueror, son of Robert "the Devil" Duke of Normandy and Arlette, a Falaisian tanner's or embalmer's daughter, was crowned King of England. He retained much Saxon law and adminis-tration, continuing to hold the "Great Meetings" at different venues on major Christian festivals.

At the Gloucester Christmas Meeting of 1085, having present his chief clerks, William ordered a national enquiry into the distribution of property. This was promptly executed, recorded particulars being brought to him before the end of 1086. These were later organized into the "Domesday Book".

Although it was carried out with such speed, the survey was too efficient for the writer of the Peterborough based Anglo-Saxon Chronicle, who lamented:— "there was not a single hide, not one virgate of land, not even — it is shameful to record, but it did not seem shameful for him to do — one ox, nor one cow, nor one pig, which escaped notice in his survey". At Peterborough at least, the survey must have been compre-hensive.

The threatened Danish invasion, which probably prompted William's action, never took place, but the survey provided, and continues to provide, an unparallelled and detailed view of the English contemporary scene. It also raises many problems for the modern investigator.

## The Domesday Manors of Olton

In the 1086 survey, the Saxon manor of Ulversleah has become Ulverlei, and Cinctune has become Cintone. The entry for Ulverlei may be translated:—

42. Land of Cristine in the Coleshelle Hundred.

Cristine holds of the king eight hides[1] in Ulverlei: land for twenty ploughs. In the desmesne[2] is one and three serfs,[3] twenty-two villeins[4] with a priest and four bordars[5] have seven ploughs. Wood four leagues[6] long and half a league wide, when it bears,[7] worth twelve shillings. Valued at ten pounds, now four pounds. Earl Edwin held it.

## i. Edwin

Edwin, Earl of Mercia, who held the manor of Ulverlei until 1071, supported his brother-in-law, King Harold, in 1066. With his brother, Morcar, he fought the Norwegian invaders at Fulford, near York, and though defeated, sufficiently weakened the enemy to make Harold's famous victory at Stamford Bridge more possible. Before the brothers could muster another army to support Harold at Senlac (Hastings), the Normans had been victorious and Harold was dead. The two invasions and three battles all took place in little more than a single month.

On William's victory, the brothers transferred their allegiance to the cause of the Saxon heir, Edgar Atheling, which was centred on London. With William's encirclement of London, the Atheling's party collapsed. Its leaders, including Edwin and Morcar, submitted to William. The brothers were attached to William's court, and, by the end of 1067, had been confirmed in their estates and were signing charters as members of the King's Council.

In 1068 relationships deteriorated and Edwin, disappointed that a promised marriage alliance with William's daughter had not been honoured, left the Court for the North, where there was considerable anti-Norman activity. Morcar accompanied his brother.

In 1071, William attempted to arrest Edwin, who escaped by hiding and afterwards fled towards Scotland. Betrayed by three of his vassals, and hindered by an ill tide which rendered a rivulet impassable, Edwin was caught and killed. His assassins, who sent his head to the king, received an unexpected "reward": they were sentenced to perpetual banishment.

Escaping by ship, Morcar joined the rebel Hereward the Wake, in the Isle of Ely. It is generally accepted that, when Morcar submitted to William with the rest of Hereward's followers, he survived, but in perpetual imprisonment.

Under these circumstances, the estates of both brothers, including Ulverlei, would, in 1071, have reverted to the king.

# THE DESCENT OF CHRISTINE

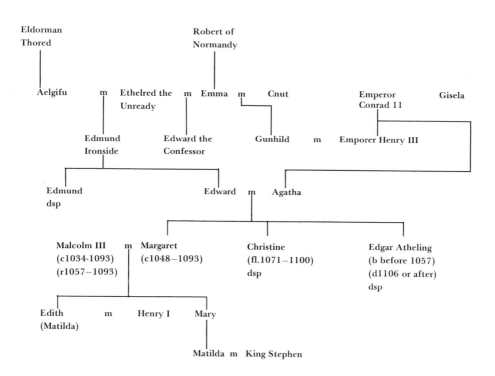

## KEY

| | | |
|---|---|---|
| m | = | Married |
| r | = | Reigned |
| fl | = | Flourished (alive between these dates) |
| b | = | Born |
| d | = | Died |
| dsp | = | Died Without Issue |

## ii Cristine

### Descent

After Edmund Ironside died in November 1016, Cnut, who then became "King of all England", sent Edmund's infant sons, Edmund and Edward, to Olave, King of Sweden. Cnut's violent nature would have given credence to the claim, made in the Worcester-based Anglo-Saxon Chronicle, that he intended that the children should be "put out of the way". Fortunately, they were, "by some means", transferred to the protection of the saintly King Stephen of Hungary (ruled 997 – 1038).

Edmund did die young, but Edward survived to marry Agatha, a relative, probably a niece, of the emperor Henry III of Germany. Their marriage produced three children, Cristine, Margaret and Edgar. (see Fig. 3 & note 8)

### The Family comes to England

Edward the Confessor's failure to produce an heir to the English throne caused concern for the succession. An envoy was sent from England to the Emperor Henry III to request the return of Edward, as the Saxon heir apparent.

In 1057, accompanied by his family, and no doubt hopeful of being acclaimed England's future king, Edward, perhaps unwisely, returned to a land controlled by the ambitious Godwins. He was well-received by the people, but "somehow" prevented from seeing his uncle, Edward the Confessor, and died mysteriously soon after his arrival. His son Edgar then became the Atheling, or Saxon heir to the throne, but, on the Confessor's death in 1066, the crown passed to Harold Godwinson and then to William the Conqueror.

### Cristine in Scotland

In the summer of 1067, shortly after Edgar Atheling's submission to William at London, Cristine fled with her brother, her sister Margaret and their mother Agatha, to Scotland. There, King Malcolm, perhaps mindful of the help he had received from England in his struggle against Macbeth, welcomed them.

Malcolm became eager to marry Margaret, but she, like Edward the Confessor, preferred celibacy. "The lady was unwilling", and "both the prince (Edgar) and his men opposed the marriage for a long time". It is possible that Edgar even left Scotland on this issue, for, when the marriage finally took place in 1070, Edgar is said to have returned to Malcolm's court.

Cristine and Ulverlei

Initially, Malcolm supported his brother-in-law's cause, but, in 1073, William invaded Scotland, forcing Malcolm to make peace. By the terms of their agreement, Malcolm became William's vassal, giving his eldest son, Duncan (the child of a previous marriage) as a hostage. It is likely that Malcolm also had to expel Edgar and his followers, for, in the next year, when William was in Normandy, Edgar "returned to Scotland from Flanders".

Being a vassal had certain advantages. In return for service and obedience, the overlord was expected to protect and provide for the vassal and his dependants. With the "man of the family", Edgar, exiled, Malcolm's unmarried sister-in-law, Cristine, was left unprotected and unprovided for. Conveniently, the Conqueror had recently repossessed the manors of Edwin of Mercia, certain of which, including Ulverlei, he was in the process of dispersing.

In the Domesday survey, Cristine is found in possession of four properties, three, Ulverlei, Arlei and Icentone (Long Itchington) in Warwickshire, and one, Bradewelle, in Oxfordshire. In the Warwickshire entries, the connection between Cristine and the King is so firmly established that the 18th century Birmingham historian, Hutton, deduced that she was his mistress, "probably a handsome lass of the same complexion as his mother". Ulverlei and Arlei (assessed together), Cristine "holds of the King" (ten. de rege). Under Icentone it states "When the King gave (it) to Cristine" (Quando Rex dedit Cristinae). It is likely that this provision for Cristine was a clause in the agreement between Malcolm and William, and that Cristine held Ulverlei from 1073 to 1086.

Ulverlei appeared in 1085/6 as a poor and depreciating holding, having decreased in value from £10 to £4, while Bradewelle (Oxon) was shown as an estate enjoying an increasing prosperity (from £25 to £30 to £31). Icentone had made some recovery, after an initial fall in value (£36 to £12 to £20). The well-being of the estates may have related to Cristine's involvement. It is unlikely that, with an alternative offered by Bradewelle, with its more considerable desmesne, extensive pasture/ meadow land and fishery, Cristine would have spent much time at Ulverlei.

Cristine at Romsey

Although Cristine still held the manor of Ulverlei at the time of the Domesday survey in 1086, she "retired into the Abbey at Romeseie and took the veil". Her surrender of the manor may have been prompted, or enforced, by a further disagreement between her brother, Edgar Atheling, and King William. Another entry for 1086 in the Anglo-

Saxon Chronicle claims: "Prince Edgar, the kinsman of King Edward, left his (William's) Court, because he had little honour from him". As her brother continued to consort with William's foes, Cristine probably adopted the safest course. She took her vows at Romsey and became Abbess there.

## Romsey Abbey

The Benedictine Abbey at Romsey, Hampshire, was founded c 910. The remains of a pre-Norman church apse have been discovered below the existing church. It was a wealthy foundation and it has been suggested that Cristine made it wealthier. Certainly, about the time of her death, the Abbey embarked on a building programme which extended through much of the 12th century. The Abbey was sold for £100 at the Dissolution, and only the church now remains. (Plate 4)

## Cristine and Edith

While Cristine was Abbess of Romsey, she was charged with the care of her niece, Edith, the daughter of Margaret and Malcolm of Scotland. According to Eadmer, Edith "only wore the veil to keep off importunate

Plate 4                                 Romsey Abbey Church, Hampshire.

16

and undesirable suitors". Henry I, who had seized the English throne on the death of his brother, William II, was not so easily deterred. He based his claim to the crown on his English origins, and sought a princess of English descent for his wife. Pious, homely, charitable and orphaned, Edith was conveniently to hand. Henry's promiscuity would not have recommended him as a husband. There was probably some opposition from Cristine, as the recently-returned Anselm, Archbishop of Canterbury, held an enquiry before the marriage was allowed to take place.

Finding Edith had worn the veil but not taken her vows, Anselm released her to marry the King. She changed her name to Matilda on her marriage and accession in 1100.

No more seems to be known about Cristine. It is assumed that she died at Romsey, some time after 1100 and certainly before 1130 when a Hadewise is recorded as Abboss. Her sister, Margaret, had died in 1093 a few days after hearing of the deaths of her husband and son in battle. The marriage, for all Margaret's initial reluctance, appears to have been successful. Margaret was canonized in 1251. Edgar Atheling survived, almost miraculously, until at least 1106 when he was still opposing the Norman King of England. He was taken prisoner at the Seige of Tinchebrai, but "let go unmolested" by Henry I. It is suggested that he lived on in retirement, either in Scotland or in Oxfordshire, where he had been an Earl under Harold.

## *Cintone*

The Domesday entry for Cintone (Kineton Green[9]) translates:

28. Land of Willi son of Corbucian
From W Ailmar holds 2 hides in Cintone. Land for 2 ploughs. There are 5 villagers who have them. Wood 1/2 league long. 4 furlongs wide. It was and is valued at 10 shillings. Turchil held it freely.
T.R.E.

## *The Tenants of Cintone*

i Turchil

The Turchil of Warwick, who is shown holding 70 properties in the Warwickshire Domesday survey, is generally accounted a Saxon. His father can be identified as Alwin, Vice-comes for Warwickshire, who is mentioned in a College of Arms charter for 1072.

In the 11th century, the family was allied to the Saxon earls of Mercia. A Turchil was slain, in company with Leofric's brother, while fighting the Welsh in 1039.    Turchil of Warwick's second marriage was with Leverunia, sister to Edwin and Morcar.

If not Turchil of Warwick himself, the Turchil who had held two hides in Cintone freely in the time of Edward the Confessor (T.R.E.) was most likely to be a near relation.

Although Saxonized, the Warwickshire Turchils probably originated from Denmark.    A Danish branch of the family was still flourishing in 1069, when "Jarl Turchil" met Edgar Atheling in the Humber estuary. The name Turchil suggests Scandinavian origins, 'Thor' being the god of thunder in Norse mythology, and 'Ketill' being old Norse for a deep food vessel, remembered in the fish kettles of the 19th and early 20th centuries.

During the 11th century, the name was variously spelt (Thurkytel, Thurkil, etc) and applied to different individuals, but a common role, that of thegn (literally "one who serves") may be discerned.    A Turchil served Edward the Confessor as a "stirman" (steersman), and "batoc" (boatman) has been inserted above the name Turchil[10] in the Warwickshire Domesday entry for Ermendone.    The rivers were the highways, and Warwick was virtaully an inland port, required to provide the king with four "batfueins" (boatmen) or £4 of pence, when the king went against his enemies by sea.

Under William the Conqueror, Turchil of Warwick received his paternal inheritance from the gift of the King (see Ingulphus).    In the survey, seven Warwickshire properties which had belonged to Alwin were added to those Turchil held in his own right.    Not only did the Conqueror allow Turchil to retain his material wealth, but also his status.    He was appointed keeper of Warwick Castle and Vice-comes of Warwickshire.

However, early in the reign of William Rufus (1087 — 1100), Dugdale asserts that the whole inheritance of Turchil, Deputy to the Earl of Mercia, was "bestowed on Henry de Newburgh".    Nevertheless, the Turchil family was not entirely impoverished, as Turchil's son, Siward, is known to have held ten knights' fees in Warwickshire.

The Warwickshire Turchils have a further claim to fame.    They can be traced as the ancestors of William Shakespeare, through his mother, Mary Arden, having at some time after the Norman Conquest changed their name to the more politcally acceptable "de Arden".

## ii The Corbucions

The 'William son of Corbucion' holding two hides in Cintone, is shown in possession of eighteen other Warwickshire estates totalling $37.^2/_3$ hides and two Warwick houses, in the 1086 survey — a much smaller property than Ralph de Limesy's.   It was at Studley, the more prosperous of the two 4-hide properties, that the family was established. William's most prominent descendant Peter, known as 'de Studley', who was active from 1166, probably built the castle there.

### Studley Castle

This castle remained in the family until the death of the last direct male heir, another Peter, in 1356.   The ruins, noted by Dugdale, have now disappeared, but the moat and site are still clearly discernible, forming the front gardens of private residences on the north side of Studley Church.   An exploratory excavation, dug across one of the ditches by Mr G.E. Saville of Alcester, produced a piece of pottery identified as twelfth century.

*Ulverley to 1213*

When Cristine retired to Romsey, William the Conqueror gave her Warwickshire estates to his putative nephew, Ralph de Limesy. Limesy is a French town approximately 15km north of Robert the Devil's castle near Rouen.

In 1086 Ralph already owned five hides in Budbrook (Warks) and houses in Warwick, as well as forty estates in other counties. The family's main seat was at Pirton, near Hitchin in Hertfordshire, but Ulverley was important as they derived the title of their barony from that manor.

Ralph, and his wife Hadewise, appear to have been committed Christians and benefactors of the Christian church. Ralph founded the church at Pirton, giving two parts of his tythes from Ulverley for its support. This early twelfth century building consisted of a chancel, nave and tower. After several alterations, it was completely restored in 1883, the tower being rebuilt from the foundations. The chancel walls are probably all that is left of the original church to which our Olton predecessors contributed. (Plate 5)

Plate 5                                         Pirton Church, Hertfordshire.

Ralph and Hadewise then transferred their interest to the Abbey of St. Albans, giving the tithes of the church at Pirton and those of the Priory of St. Mary in Hertford (which Ralph had founded as a cell to St. Albans) with 'divers lands and tythes' to that monastery. In return, the monks of St. Albans accepted Ralph and Hadewise as 'brother' and 'sister', thereby assuring them of burial and prayers for their souls.

Their descendants made further gifts to the Church. From Alan, their son, the Priory of Hertford received the tithes of the Church of Long Itchington (Cristine's Icentone), to which Gerard, his son, added a "grass-croft" in Long Itchington, amongst other property. The grateful monks were "to pray for his soul and the souls of Amy (Alice) his wife, and John his son.

John died in 1198. His only son, Hugh, died without issue and the Limesy estates passed to John's sisters, Basilia and Eleanor, for which, in 1211, a substantial "fine" of five hundred marks was levied by King John. Ulverley came to Basilia, and her husband Hugh de Odingsels, whom she married in 1213. He was the son of William, a "miles" (soldier), and the grandson of Hugh, who had come from Flanders.

## THE KINGS OF ENGLAND, 1066 — 1307

| | | |
|---|---|---|
| William I | (The Conqueror) | 1066 — 1087 |
| William II | (Rufus) | 1087 — 1100 |
| Henry I | (Beauclerk) | 1100 — 1135 |
| Stephen | | 1135 — 1154 |
| Henry II | | 1154 — 1189 |
| Richard I | (Lionheart) | 1189 — 1199 |
| John | (Lackland) | 1199 — 1216 |
| Henry III | | 1216 — 1272 |
| Edward I | | 1272 — 1307 |

*The Church in the twelfth century*

The religious revival under Henry I (1100 — 1135) in which Ralph de Limesy and Hadewise had participated, with its extensions of existing buildings, new religious foundations and the introduction of stricter orders, was interrupted by the civil war between Stephen and Matilda, who contended for Henry I's crown. It was continued after the stettlement, doubtless aided by 'conscience money' from the more moral of those who had used the breakdown of order for personal gain. Once more it became fashionable to found and endow religious houses.

Pious enthusiasm was generated by the Crusades, 'holy' wars fought by Christians from 1096 to 1291, to regain and hold the Holy Land. The Knights Templars, a fighting order of monks associated with the Crusades and introduced into England by Matilda herself, was the recipient of many gifts of land. A local 'Temple' was established at Temple Balsall during the reign of Stephen.

## Knights and Priors

In accordance with the fashion, and possibly following his own inclination and conception of duty, William son of Corbucion's descendant, Peter de Studley, contributed generously to the Christian Church. Before 1185, he gave lands and a mill to the Knights Templars. He established a priory of Austin Canons at Wicton (Worcestershire) which he endowed with lands, woods and a mill. These were transferred to Studley, where he founded the Priory during the reign of Henry II (1154 – 1189).

There are implications that by this time the term "gift" had become euphemistic. Henry II himself extracted "gifts" from the then wealthy Church. These were given under protest and it is likely that certain religious establishments, in order to recoup their losses, practised the same type of extortion on their landed devotees and tenants. The facts that certain "gifts" given by Peter were contested by his descendants and that no services appear to have been rendered in exchange by the religious foundations, suggest that, unlike the Limesys' gifts, those of the Corbucions may have been of this order.

Certainly the Corbucion properties came under strain, and, as the Corbucion family was reduced, the Priors of Studley increased in wealth and importance. View of frankpledge,[1] and assize of bread and ale[2] were granted to the Prior, as to the Lord of the Manor. By 1316, the Prior of Studley was accounted "one of the chief lords", while the contemporary Peter Corbucion (no longer 'de Studley') was merely "one of the lords". After the Dissolution[3] (1538) when the Priory estate passed to Edmund Knightly, it was accounted the chief manor of Studley.

## Feudalism

### i The Feudal System

With the creation of the first Anglo-Norman Earl, Henry de Newburgh, at Warwick, William the Conqueror established his organization of England, conveniently known as the Feudal System. It was essentially a rationalization and extension of the Saxon King/thegn/peasant relationships. "Barons"[4] held their large estates as tenants-in-chief from the King. Their surplus land was divided amongst subtanants.    Below these was a variety of poor, ranging from those who held their own land to slaves, who did not even own themselves.

## ii  Conditions of Tenure

The rent for peasants was food and labour:  for the barons, attendance on the King in Council and war, when, and as, summoned.  "Relief" could be exacted on the succession of an heir.  If that heir were a minor, the overlord, King or baron, could hold and enjoy profits from his estate. The King could demand "aids", the chief of these being paid for the King's ransom, if captured, the marriage of his eldest daughter and the knighting of his eldest son.

The system was enforced by threats of dispossession and distraint. King John (1195 — 1216) also introduced "fines", levied before a battle on those who failed to attend, and even on those whose services were not required.

## iii  Knights' Fees

By 1135, most of the Domesday properties had been converted into holdings, variable in size and value, known as Knights' Fees.  These were usually held by a sub-tenant under a baron.  For each fee, the services of an armed man were required by the King, in addition to the usual feudal dues.    This led to the emergence of a fighting class known as "knights".[5]

## iv The Knight of Cintone

When Henry II ordered a return of all holdings from his tenants-in-chief, in anticipation of his eldest daughter's wedding, the Earl of Warwick included Peter de Studley as holding ten knights' fees in Warwickshire. By calculation, it is almost certain that the two Domesday hides in Cintone constituted one of these knights' fees.  By 1166, both Peter de Studley and Cintone were firmly established in the Feudal System.

## v The Demise of Feudalism

Serious cracks in feudalism had become apparent during the late twelfth century.  Barons and knights showed an increasing reluctance, or inability, to implement the system.  Both classes consisted of landed tenants.  The demands of land and warfare competed for their attention over the summer months, and scutage (payment in lieu), in force by 1100, was increasingly used as an alternative to personal service.

However, successive kings' assessments of scutage per knight's fee were arbitrary and frequently considered excessive.  In 1196, most lay and church 'barons' accepted the Crown's offer of a single high payment, to be recouped from their under tenants. This solution was not necessarily a happy one for the latter.

## vi Knights in Distress

Although the wealthy 'towns' were taxed in 1177, the bulk of England's revenue still came from the landed tenants. The costs of Richard I's crusade, with an army "almost continuously in the field", his ransom of 150,000 marks[6] — twice the Country's total annual revenue, Henry III's expensive and badly-organized Gascon Campaign, the Welsh Wars and the Barons' rebellion, all took their toll.

A tax on moveables (salary, rents and chattels) akin to modern income tax, introduced to meet the costs of the Crusade and ransom, did not exclude the landed tenant. Danegeld, a land tax introduced by Ethelred to bribe the Danes, was exacted until at least 1170. Carucage, a tax on ploughed land (caracu = plough) was imposed with growing frequency towards the end of the twelfth century.

During the following century, tenants and knights' fees were further burdened by the rising costs of arming a knight. This was partly due to inflation, so rife at the beginning of the century that King John returned the Royal estates to payment in kind, but also to the increasingly sophisticated plate armour which was replacing the chain mail of the old Norman "miles". (see Figs 4 & 5)

The more heavily armoured man required a great war horse to bear him. These, at £40 to £80 each in contemporary currency, were valuable enough to warrant expensive protective armour for the horse, which raised the cost still higher. Scutage was increased accordingly.

The twelfth and thirteenth centuries were not propitious for the non-militant tenant of several small knights' fees. It is hardly surprising that under such social and economic pressures, Peter de Studley's holdings were dispersed. Eventually, most of what remained of the Corbucion estates, probably including Cintone, came into the hands of the de Montforts of Beaudesert, kinsfolk of the Earl of Warwick. Again "gifts" were in evidence, either to the de Montforts themselves,. or to the Cantilupes, who had associations with the family. A William de Cantilupe was guardian to Peter de Montfort, a minor (1216 – 1227).

## The de Montforts of Beaudesert

Thurstan de Montfort, great nephew of Henry de Newburgh, was established at Beaudesert by 1140. This branch of the de Montfort

24

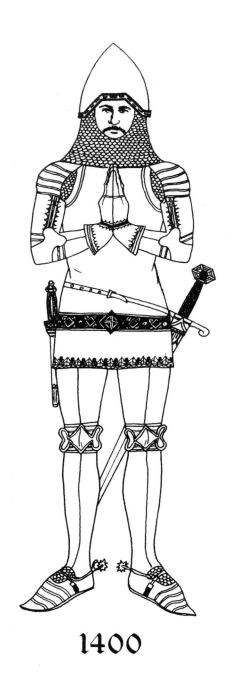

# 1400

Plate Armour
Fig. 4

**1414**

Plate Armour
Fig 5

family rose to prominence with Peter, who died fighting with his cousin Simon at the Battle of Evesham in 1265.

After his victory over the rebel barons,[7] Henry III proceeded with the repossession and in some cases the redistribution of their properties, but the alienation of established families and the disposal of land on such a scale was obviously undesirable, if not impossible. The Dictum of Kenilworth, an expedient measure, outlined the ways by which estates might be recovered for fines and renewed allegiance.

Peter de Montfort's estates, with the possible exception of Cintone, were returned to his heir. Eventually, with the failure of the male line, the de Montfort properties passed through the Earls of Warwick to the Botelers of Sudeley.

## Cintone Returns to the King

Edward I succeeded his father, Henry III in 1272. He had married Eleanor of Castile, then a child, in 1254. As Queen of England, a legal provision ("dowry") had to be made for her by Edward.

This dowry, listed in a Charter Roll[8] for 1275, includes the "farms" (a composite of all dues, tolls, tithes etc.) of 'Kinton'. On her death, this was to revert 'to the King's heirs and not be alienated from the Crown', and when, after her death in 1290, many of her possessions were given to the Church of St Peter, Westminster, to provide for her soul, 'Kinton' was not included.

## King's Knight

While the Corbucions declined under Feudalism, the Odingsels flourished. Hugh and Basilia held the Barony of Ulverley, and part of Pirton "by knight service". Hugh was a professional soldier loyal to the Crown, at a time when such individuals were in demand.

When the nine year old Henry III came to the throne in 1216, most of Eastern England was in the hands of Louis, later the VIII, of France. A long struggle to regain Henry's castles commenced, and, in 1221, Hugh "attended" the young king at the seige of Bitham Castle (Lincs) bringing with him a considerable band of followers.

On Hugh's death (1238), his younger son, William, inherited Ulverley, and held it on the same terms. Matthew Paris referred to him as a 'miles strennus', a title he appears to have earned. In 1242 he attended King Henry III on his Gascon Campaign, though Gerard, his elder brother, preferred to pay 50 marks scutage. William also supported Henry III against the Welsh (1249, 1250 and 1260), and in 1263 against the de Montforts at the beginning of the Barons' War.

Wisely, the Odingsels withdrew their allegiance from the over-burdened and depreciating countryside, and concentrated on Solihull, a new settlement first mentioned in the reign of John (1199 – 1216). Under William de Odingsel who, in 1242 gained for it a weekly market and annual fair, Solihull grew in importance.

William was personally rewarded by being given the Governorship of Montgomery Castle (1249), exclusive hunting rights all over his desmesne (1250), and an annuity of 30 marks "until better provision should be made" (1261).

It was unlikely that better provision was ever made. Four years later he was dead, and his Ulverley/Solihull estate came to his elder son, also William, who continued the family's military tradition, fighting for the King against Simon de Montfort and the barons, the Welsh, and in Ireland. There he was rewarded in 1294 with all the land and castle of Donymegan in Connaught, as "a gift for good service". He was knighted in 1283.

In Solihull, Sir William established the machinery of law, a Court, gallows, tumbrel and assize for bread and beer. In 1288 he built the Chantry [9] 'for the health of his parents', progenitors' and children's souls'.

It was almost certainly Sir William who moved across the heath to establish the Odingsels' new manor house known as Silhill Hall, wantonly destroyed in 1966. This move was probably prompted by his marriage to Ela, youngest daughter of William Longspee (long sword), second Earl of Salisbury. Her grandfather, also William Longspee, was the putative son of King Henry II and the "Fair Rosamund" about whom many romantic stories grew. One local legend concerns the Fair Rosamund Cup. This supposedly came to the Wilsons of Knowle in 1716, from the Sheppards of Great Rollright, and was inscribed

"Fair Rosamund's cup
A Wilson shall hold
So long as a Wilson
Is faithful and bold"

On Sir William's death in 1295, the estates were divided amongst his four daughters. The manor of "Oulton" fell to Margaret and her husband, Sir John Grey of Rotherfield (d 1311). A Close Roll of 1292 recorded that the "hamlet of Hulverlee", together with the Manor of Knowle and other properties, was held by the Church of St Peter, Westminster, with "return of writs and all liberties and free customs which they have in their other lands", for the ease of Queen Eleanor's soul.

28

This suggests that "Oulton" and "Hulverlee" co-existed as separate settlements, and that "Olton" is not, as often believed, a new name applied to the old estate of Ulverley.

## The Dispute over the Chapels of Lyndon and Kington (Cintone)

Estates were not divided only on the failure of the male line. Pressures on Knights' Fees caused subdivisions of up to one hundred parts. The rights and dues and land of a single manor could be split and then subdivided amongst different individuals and religious houses. The right to a peasant's labour might be separated from that to his rents. The growing use of money led to land purchase so that scattered parcels of land fell to different owners. In 1291, for example, Robert de Someri, Baron Dudley, held one manor and one pasture in Olton. Such divisions not only create problems for modern investigation but generated a certain amount of contemporary confusion, as in the dispute over Cintone Church.

In 1199, Henry le Notte held one virgate (c 30 acres) of land in Kingsford and Kington (Cintone).[10] In 1221, a Henry le Notte gave the advowson (right to appoint a priest) of the Church at Kington to Markyate Priory. This Benedictine house had been established in Bedfordshire c 1145 under the Abbot of St Albans. After Henry le Notte's gift, the nuns there acquired Lyndon Chapel and extended the advowson of Kington to a full possession of the Church. When the Prior of St Mary's Kenilworth pleaded poverty, the Crown, which had regained Cintone on the death of Queen Eleanor, granted him in 1314 the "Church of Kintona" (Charter Roll). This was contested by the nuns of Markyate who "endeavoured to establish their rights to the dependant chapels of Cintone and Lyndon". In 1329 judgement was given for the nuns, and the churches remained with Markyate throughout problems of poverty and charges of immorality and broken vows.

The poor state of the Priory was doubtless reflected in that its dependant chapels, one of which it had been ordered to repair in 1296. Markyate was surrendered by the Church authorities in 1536, prior to Henry VIII's general enforcement and probably with some relief. Its total possessions were valued at £155.5.10¾. It is possible that the closure of the Priory was followed by the decay of the chapels at Lyndon and Kineton, as Bickenhill and Solihull became the religious centres for the area.

## The Parish of Bickenhill

The Priory of Markyate was found possessed, at its surrender, of the titles of Coleshill, Bickenhill and three chapels in Warwickshire. The third Warwickshire Chapel's being Bickenhill would explain how Lyndon and Kineton came to be in Bickenhill Parish during the 13th century. A parish, at that time, was a loose association of churches administered by one priest. Markyate Priory would have appointed a single priest for its three Warwickshire chapels. The survival of the church at Bickenhill would result in that church's pastoral responsibility for the whole area.

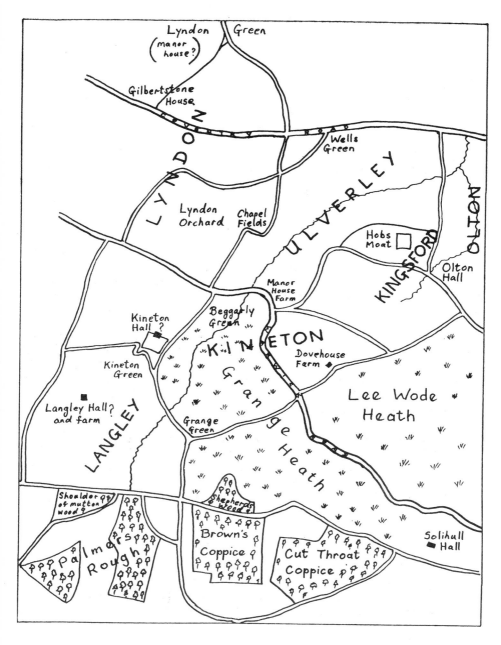

Sketch map of the six settlements

Fig. 6

# CHAPTER 4: FARMHOUSES, HALLS AND HEATHS

While Solihull became more urbanized, the area now known as Olton remained rural, consisting of heaths, woods, farms, cottages and the occasional hall or large house. Farming and allied pursuits, such as tanning or hunting, became the main occupations of its residents. This state of affairs is clearly reflected in the 1841 Census, where, apart from a few 'independents' and the School Master with fifteen scholars at Bradford House, the bulk of the population is shown consisting of farmers, agricultural labourers, household servants and leather dressers.

*The New Settlements*

i Kingsford

Four apparently new settlements emerged after the Domesday Survey. These were Kingsford, Lyndon, Langley [1] and Olton. Kingsford is mentioned as early as 1199, and it is possible, from its name and position, that this was a part of Cintone not recorded in the Domesday Book.

Kingsford came into prominence in the late 16th and early 17th centuries with the James family, several of whom were buried in Solihull Church. Thomas James (1668 – 1741) was one of the gentry who refused to make a financial contribution towards the production of Henry Beighton's map of Warwickshire (1725). Consequently, his shield in the border decoration remained blank.

By his wife Elizabeth, Thomas had two daughters, Mary, who died aged 12 in 1717, and Elizabeth, who married Edward Knight of Cookley (Worcs). Her son, Richard, died aged 14, the family appears to have come to an end and Kingsford, as a separate entity, disappeared from the Warwickshire maps.

ii Lyndon

When Markyate Priory proved its right to the chapel at Lyndon, that settlement must have been already well established. It may have had a manor house as early as 1221. Certainly, in 1468, when a court was held there by Thomas Palmer and his wife Elizabeth Bishopsdon, it was a manor in its own right. In 1631, the manor was sold to the Devereux of Castle Bromwich.

The boundaries of Lyndon extended beyond the Coventry Road, into what is now Birmingham. It is likely that Lyndon Manor House was situated near the junction of Barrow's Lane and Manor House Lane, where there is still an area known as Lyndon Green.

The memory of the Old Chapel has been preserved through three centuries by map references varying from Chapel Yard (a yard was a measure of land) and Chapel Fields in the 18th century to Chapel Fields Farm in the 19th century and Chapel Fields Road and Schools, today.

## iii Langley

Langley may have been settled during the land development urged by central government to accommodate the rising population of the 13th century. It was mentioned in 1295 when "Alice de Langley is said to have called herself Lady of Bickenhill", and it appears regularly on maps throughout the 18th century.

Langley Hall is shown by Beighton as an "old house" in 1725, being represented by his Elizabethan symbol. The farm survived or super-ceeded the Hall and in 1841 was occupied by Elizabeth Lowe, aged 35, Henry Lowe, aged 25, farmers and their five servants. The Hall is remembered in Langley Hall Road. Robin Hood Golf Course and the Langley Schools now cover the old Hall and farm land.

## iv Olton

Of all the divisions, 'Oulton' became the most important. The name occurs in 1291 and again in 1295 when Sir William Odingsel and his wife Ela Longspee jointly held the manor of Oulton. In a 'fine' of 1467 it is precisely placed "juxta (abutting) Solyhull". It stretched from that village to include Olton Hall just within its boundaries.

The descent of Olton Manor from Sir William Odingsel to the Palmer family is given by Dugdale (Antiquities of Warwickshire) and Pemberton (Solihull and its Church).

## The Palmers of Olton

By 1604, when Ann Palmer was baptized at Solihull Church, the Palmers were living at Olton Hall which, after 1623 when divisions called 'ends' were introduced for the maintenance of roads, became known as Olton End Hall. Henry Palmer married Ann Greswolde of Greet (1631 — 1669). Of their nine children, only three married, Mary to William Makepeace, Benjamin to Ann Grimshaw and Elizabeth to Thomas Doley. Elizabeth's husband died in 1704. One of her daughters died 17 months later, but the other, Ann, lived to marry William Shepherd of Rollright.

The Palmers were a charitable family.  Henry gave 20 shillings "mill money" for four poor widows.  Martha, his daughter, who died in 1723, left £50 for educating poor girls, and Thomas Doley gave Berry Fields, amongst other property, to "provide poor boys with clothing".

Olton Hall Estate came to Henry's youngest son, Benjamin, and then to his grandson, also Benjamin, the last and best known of the Palmers.

There is a bust of this Benjamin Palmer in Solihull Church, and a description of him by Hutton, the Birmingham historian.  After an unflattering account of his physical appearance — "He measured about 5'5" tall, but was singularly short in the lower parts and was as immoderately heavy as he was tall", "He seemingly dozed as he walked", and "as a man he shone by his bulk" — Hutton begrudgingly allows Benjamin Palmer some integrity, if not much wisdom — "As a magistrate he shone in a dull but honest light — his decisions were intended to be just". Benjamin extended the Palmer property to include the Knowle Hall Estate, which he purchased from the widow of Francis Smith, the Warwick architect, in 1754.  The Hall itself, reputedly built by Inigo Jones, was demolished at the end of the 19th. century.

He had married Elizabeth Knight, some 17 years his junior.  They had no children, and on Benjamin's death, Elizabeth married Mr Charles Baldwin of Shropshire, whom she also survived.  Though she died in London in 1812, forty years after the death of her first husband, she was buried by his side in the Palmer vault in Solihull Church.

Mrs Baldwin had held the Palmer estates in trust, and on her death they were shared between Jane Wilson, a descendant of Thomas Doley and Elizabeth Palmer via the Sheppards of Rollright, and Henry Greswolde Lewis of Malvern Hall, a descendant of William Makepeace and Mary Palmer.  Olton Hall came to Henry Lewis who on his death left his property to his cousins, the Wigleys and the Wilsons.  By an Act of Parliament, the co-heirs obtained permission to divide the estates. Knowle went to the Wilsons, Malvern and Olton Halls went to the Wigleys.

The three unmarried Wigleys, Caroline, Edmund and Meysey, settled at Malvern Hall, but disaster struck.  Meysey, a clergyman, died after "drinking freely" with his cousin, "Gumley" Wilson, amongst others, and falling downstairs.  In 1833 Edmund Wigley died suddenly while with the army in Ireland.  His death brought financial problems for the family, as he had relied on insurance policies, which were not honoured, to settle his debts.  Malvern Hall had to be handed over to an uncle and Caroline inherited Olton.

An attack of infantile paralysis had left Caroline in leg-irons, but this did not prevent her from leading an active life. She travelled abroad and was one of the few women of her time to hold a public office (Surveyor of the Highways).

She also rebuilt Olton Hall. When the new hall was sold as part of the Elmdon Hall Estate, it was reported to be built on the remains of a much older residence, with woodwork and panelling which had been removed from Henwood Priory. (Plate 6)

Caroline found her "fairy prince" in the Rev Archer Clive, Vicar of Solihull. The general amazement at the match was expressed by J Waddington, a servant at Knowle Hall, in a letter to his friend:

> "and she got married to the clergyman at Solihull, a very rich man, and a good match for her, poor creature, for she was a perfect cripple — all people were astonished — however a cripple or not a cripple, a husband must be had."

A very different story emerges from the diaries and letters of Archer and Caroline.

Plate 6        Olton Hall, rebuilt in the 19th century by Caroline Wigley.

The wedding had taken place in 1840, and "thus Olton Hall was at liberty and Mr Wilson has took it" continued J Waddington, writing in 1841. This Mr Wilson was "Gumley", Caroline's rakish cousin who had been present at the Malvern Hall drinking party. He took Olton Hall furnished for £260 p.a. for 21 years, besides "two newly built cottages for £8". Before the 21 years were up, "Gumley" was bankrupt, and in America under a new name.

Amongst the Wilson pictures which "disappeared", there were reputed to be portraits of Henry, Ann, Benjamin Palmer II, and Benjamin Palmer I "with his family, pack of hounds and Olton End Hall".

An Olton Hall still stands on Lode Lane. It was made into a public house, and is now The Newport Diner.

*The Original Settlements*

i Kineton

Cintone emerges as Kineton, a village at the junction of Brook Lane and Kineton Green Road. Here stood Kineton Hall, cottages and probably the chapel. The settlement can be seen in the remnant of the Green (Plate 7), the yew tree 250–300 years old and the oaks of similar age which line Kineton Green Road — the road to the village from the Kineton turnpike (Warwick Road from Acocks Green to St Margaret's Church) and Streetsbrook Road, and in the way Brook Lane bends, as though to avoid previously established buildings.

Plate 7                                           All that remains of Kineton Green.

Near the old yew tree, two timber framed brick cottages survived until after the last war. One was restored by Mr Rose, a retired art teacher, who believed that the timber framework dated from the 13th century. A survey of the cottages revealed one unfit for human habitation, and they were both demolished to make way for new houses.

Although Kineton Hall appears on maps until 1860, the labelling is so imprecise it is impossible to identify its exact location. The 1839 tythe map shows a "homestead yard and garden" (900) on the Yew tree corner, which may have been the Hall. The Le Nottes, who gave the advowson of the church to Markyate, are reputed to have lived at the Hall for about 200 years.

ii Ulverley

Ulverley probably remained in the control of the monks of St Peter's Westminster until the Dissolution. It appears as a narrow strip separating Olton from Lyndon. Its last substantial building appears to have been Manor House Farm, reputed to have been built on the site of the old manor house and entered as Ulverley Hall Farm (lot 30) in the Elmdon Estate Sale Catalogue (Plate 8) In the same catalogue, the Club House and golf course (lot 7) are placed at "Ulverley Green" near Olton, which suggests that Ulverley preserved some independence even into this century.

Plate 8                                    Manor Farm circa 1900.

Apart from its six settlements, the area had many scattered farms, woods and two heaths. Grange Heath stretched over Grange Road, probably including World's End and the marsh which is now Olton Reservoir. Two remnants of this heath, Beggarly Green, between the reservoir and the Warwick Road, and Grange Green at the junction of Kineton Green Road, St Bernard's Road and Grange Road, survived into the 19th century.

The second heath was probably initially sheltered woodland known as Lee Wood. It stretched from the Warwick Road across to Lode Lane, and became known as Lewd Heath or Lode Heath, possibly as the woodland was reduced.

About Streetsbrook Road, the reminders of woodland — Palmer's Rough, (Plate 9&10) Brown's Coppice, Cut-throat Coppice, Pow Grove, Shepherd's Wood and Shoulder of Mutton Wood — argue substantial afforestation. It has been suggested that this was one edge of the great Forest of Arden.

Plate 9        Palmer's Rough as it is today.

Plate 10     Palmer's Close — the name a reminder of an ancient woodland.

The many Robin Hood references also echo woodland associations. Sherriff's map (1788 — 96) shows Robin Hood's Ways. These could have been the pathways by which earlier inhabitants came to the Robin Hood rites.

Gradually, the waste land was reduced, an amalgam of the six settlements became known as Olton, and the area stood poised for the urban development of the nineteenth and twentieth centuries.

c  Jean Powrie

# NOTES (Chapters 1 — 4 inclusive)

## CHAPTER 1

1. Erratics : Large rocks brought from a distance by a glacier.
2. From information provided by Dr. Prag, Keeper of Archaeology, Manchester Museum.
3. c. (circa) approximately.

## CHAPTER 2

1. Hide : An area of land, varying from place to place, assessed at 120 acres maximum.   A virgate (Latin) or yardland (Old English) was usually ¼ hide.
2. Desmesne : That part of an estate reserved for the lord's use.

3/4 Serfs, villeins : slaves.

5. Border : A smallholder.
6. League : The 'Domesday' league was reckoned 1½ miles.
7. 'When it bears' : i.e. mast, the fruit of forest trees used for pig food.
8. Cristine, Margaret and Edgar : Neither in the text, nor in fig.2, are the siblings consciously placed in order of birth.   Their relative ages are uncertain.   As he is referred to in the Anglo-Saxon Chronicles as 'The Child', Edgar is often considered the youngest.   However, it is likely that this was his title as heir apparent (the Queen was the Lady) rather than an indication of age.   Gaimer ('Church Historians of England') claimed Edgar was the eldest.
9. Kineton Green : In the past there has been some confusion over the placing of the Domesday manor of Cintone.   At least two maps, purporting to show the geography of the Warwickshire Domesday manors, have identified it with Kineton, placing it together with a Longelie, near Edgehill.   The descents of the manors demonstrate that Cintone and Kineton are not the same.
10. Turchil : Not necessarily the Turchil of Cintone.

## CHAPTER 3

1. Frankpledge : A system by which, in a group of ten households, each member was responsible for the good behaviour of every other.
2. Assize of bread and ale : The power to fix the prices of these commodities.
3. The Dissolution : The closure of religious houses by Henry VIII. The larger were generally closed in 1537 and the smaller in 1538.

4. Barons : The term 'baron' was introduced at the Conquest to denote 'the man' (i.e. one who has paid homage). It was solely connected with land tenure and could apply to Abbots, Priors and secular lords. By 1164 some distinction was made between lesser and greater barons — the former holding their land from the latter and the latter holding theirs of the King. Hereditary baronies were probably introduced by Edward I.

5. Knights : Initially armed, mailed men provided for the King's service, but then, also, a special title. This could be bestowed at a public ceremony (the Accolade) until the 16th. century, or on the field, before or after a battle (11th. to 16th. centuries).

6. Mark : In England not a coin, but a money of account. After the Conquest 1 mark = 8oz. = 160 pennies = £$^2/_3$

7. The Barons' Rebellion of War : English civil war 1263 — 1267. Led by Simon de Montfort, the King's brother-in-law, a section of the barons took up arms against King Henry III and his son, later Edward I. De Montfort was defeated and killed at Evesham.

8. Rolls (Charter, Patent, Close) : Rolls were state documents, rolled for storage.

9. Chantry : An endowment for priest(s) to sing masses for the soul or the altar or chapel so endowed.

10. From 'Richard son of Richard' : Unidentified, but a 'Ricardum de Kineton' was involved in a dispute over possession in 1229 (Patent Roll).

*CHAPTER 4*

1. Langley : There seems no valid reason to associate this area with the Longelei of the Domesday Survey.

---

## HOB'S MOAT

As the archaeological exploration of Hob's Moat, now in progress, may affect previously held theories, it was considered unadvisable to include any reference to the site in the text.

A history of Olton, however, would be incomplete without some acknowledgement of such an important and unusual local earthwork, so Stuart Nichols and Gary Taylor have kindly contributed an interim report on the excavations, to be included as an appendix.

## The Excavations at Hobs Moat

The information contained below represents the current interpretive thoughts of the excavation team and may be altered in the light of further excavation.

### HOBS MOAT   MARCH 1986.

### Introduction

The impressive earthwork 'Hobs Moat' comprises a double ramparted (internal and external) moated platform covering some six acres overall. Excavations began in October 1985 and were instigated for two main reasons: the first being an attempt to save the monument from the population pressures which have extensively damaged the bank and ditch over the last 30 years. This operation involves a pure landscaping and stabilising programme under archaeological control. The second element is purely archaeological in nature and is intended to answer the initial question of what stood on this mediaeval moated site and how it fits into the overall mediaeval landscape of Solihull.

The initial work on the site concentrated on scrub clearance, and research into the documentary evidence of Hobs Moat. Whilst the former activity was completely successful, the latter, was spectacularly unsuccessful, for there appears to be no mention of Hobs Moat in the mediaeval record. This initially appeared somewhat puzzling as the site is large and might represent the settlement of a high status notable. Later thoughts on this problem have concluded that the moat probably changed its name in the mediaeval period, and as a result may be lost to the historical researcher for all time. Consequently the only way to find out the necessary information was to resort to full scale excavation.

### The site and its environs

Hobs Moat lies within an urban environment (grid reference SP.146. 826) in the Metropolitan Borough of Solihull. Situated on the geological boundary between the glacial boulder clays and keuper marls, it has a commanding topographical position which would have had an extensive view over an open landscape.

There is a remnant of green lane running along the northern side of the moat; on hedgerow-dating this should be about 650 years old. The lane branched from Castle Lane, which runs to the south of Hobs Moat, and which itself is mentioned in a document of 1339.

It is against this background that excavation commenced.  This was concentrated for the first year on three areas:—

1.  the ditch and bank.
2.  an open area, sited at the southern end of the platform where archaeological prospection surveys had indicated the possibility of buried remains, (survey undertaken by the Department of Geology, University of Birmingham)
3.  one of the possible two entrances to the site.

## The Platform Excavation

A trench was opened up that extends to 17 metres x 14 metres, and was to be excavated by the open area technique.  It soon became apparent that lying just beneath the leaf-mould and main root activity was a disturbed floor of clay.  This was evidenced by the existence of a series of clay lines which were overlain by occupation debris.  The floor is bounded by what appears to be small postholes 30cm in diameter located in construction slots.  Although these posts do not surround the whole floor, root disturbance, which has slighted the western end of the building, may be responsible for their absence.  An internal partition runs down the centre of the structure, north to south, which, like the external walls was probably constructed of planking or wattle and daub panels located between timber posts.

Fragments of probable 13th century cooking pot have been recovered from the area but do not come from sealed contexts and cannot with confidence be ascribed to the building.

Post-mediaeval activity (perhaps the agriculture mentioned by Hutton in 1783) has also left remains in this area in the form of pot sherds and clay pipe.  A fragment of the rim of a black-glazed ? cup of late 16th/early 17th century date and a rim sherd of a mottled-ware storage vessel of the 17th or 18th century have been recovered.  In addition, a clay-pipe bowl of the period 1640—80 and stamped with the maker's initials, R.N. or B.N., has also been found.

## The ditch and bank

As part of the initial excavation phase it was considered necessary to locate a trench through the ditch and both banks, this would need to be 4 metres wide, consequently, due to the tree cover only one area of the bank could be found and that was in the western rampart.  The inner bank was longitudinal sectioned and over 70 differential dumping patterns were identified.  These showed a deliberate construction strategy in order to stabilise the inner bank.  The moat-facing side has

43

been noticeably eroded; similarly, the crown of the rampart is lower than it must have originally been. However, as far as can be ascertained, it was never surmounted by a palisade fence or wall.

Beneath the present rampart an earlier bank has been discovered. No dating evidence is yet available for this, nor the present rampart, although there are two reasons to suggest that this earlier bank could belong to an altogether pre-existing earthwork. Firstly, the early bank is set well back from the crown of the present rampart. If the initial bank was related to this later feature, then it would be generally expected that one bank would sit directly beneath the other and form the core of the later rampart. The second and more convincing point is that the early bank appears to bend, particularly at its southern end, towards the moat, an orientation clearly not respected by the later visible rampart.

## *The possible entrance*

During the course of pre-excavation work two entrance-ways were identified in the inner-eastern section of the bank. It had been decided to excavate both of these eventually and therefore in order not to inhibit public access, the least passable area in the northern half of the bank was chosen. Due to the identification of dressed sandstone beneath the roots of a tree, it had already been established that the possibility of a wall existed in the immediate vicinity.

A trench was opened 8 metres x 8 metres and this revealed a confusing picture of construction and demolition. Later in the sequence there is an area of cobbling two metres x two metres running at a slight angle east to west from the edge of the bank/ditch interface. Dating evidence comes in the form of one sherd of green glazed pottery having a vertical strip decoration. The piece is tentatively dated to the 14th century, and may suggest an earliest date for the deposition of the cobbles.

A linear feature of keuper marl blocks just recently revealed, together with a tumble of cobbles, has the appearance of a wall in a state of collapse. The significance of this wall, if this is the correct interpretation, is as yet undetermined, but possibilities include a revetment to retain the rampart, or part of a structure placed in the gap in the rampart. A fragment of dressed sandstone, carved with grooves, gives a tantalizing indication of a masonry structure, perhaps of some elaboration, within this area or the immediate vicinity.

To date, this is the factual information available to the excavation team, and represents the restricted winter activities which have been severely hampered by adverse weather conditions.

The moat is featured in the section title page                    G.J. TAYLOR, B.A.

P.S. NICHOLS, B.A., A.I.F.A.

# VICTORIAN HEYDAY

*by   Margaret   Jordan*

The 1839 Tithe Map of the Lyndon Quarter of Bickenhill gives a good impression of the area and its community at that time. The parish was divided horizontally by two Turnpike roads and the canal.

The old road to Warwick had taken a route along what is now Ulverley Green Road and Ulverley Crescent, and residents in Ulverley Crescent remember an old building, demolished in 1939, that was said to have been an Elizabethan coaching inn. There was also a blacksmith, and nearby a gravel pit which could have provided roadstone.

The Warwick Turnpike road (the A41) was created in 1725. Turnpike roads were named after the barrier put across the highway to stop traffic until the toll had been paid. They were introduced in the late 17th century to provide better roads for the increased wheeled traffic and place the cost of maintenance on the road user.

Turnpike roads were not popular for although they made improvements, travellers resented paying tolls. The Elmdon Turnpike (1744) now the Coventry road was the second main road across the parish and like the Warwick Turnpike it was often in financial difficulties. Both were dissolved in 1872.

*The Grand Union Canal* (Plate 11) which follows the line of the Warwick Road through the Lyndon Quarter was opened in December 1799. It was known at first as the Birmingham to Warwick canal and ran from the Digbeth Branch of the Birmingham Canal to Warwick. It

Plate 11          The Canal from Lincoln Road bridge taken in 1904.

rises at Camp Hill by six locks to Bordesley (its summit which it maintains for 10 miles to Knowle) then by six falling locks, through Shrewley Tunnel (433 yards long) to Hatton and on to Saltisford Wharf to Warwick.

There had been opposition to the canal from land and mill owners who were concerned about a threat to their water supplies. A large influx of workers must have brought problems to the local community. The canal company employed masons, bricklayers, smiths and carpenters to build bridges and locks and hundreds of navvies to do the labouring. These men lived in barrack-like accommodation which moved as the canal building progressed. However, the coming of the canal seems to have had little effect on the rural life of the area once it was completed.

The passage of a boat through the canal system uses up large quantities of water. Natural streams were diverted as feeders, but the main water supply for the Birmingham to Warwick Canal was *Olton Reservoir* (Plate 12) constructed at the same time as the canal. The reservoir was made in a damp valley fed by Folly Brook (now Hatchford Brook) employing a technique known as "puddling". This involves kneading together clay, sand and water to make a semi-fluid puddle which is applied in two or three layers. These layers were literally trodden down by the workmen to the base of the reservoir to make it watertight. This work is said to have been done by Napoleonic prisoners of war though there is no proof of this.

Though the canals carried large volumes of goods more economically than road transport their great defect was slowness. Plans were authorised for the *Birmingham and Oxford railway* by 1846. It's main objective was a link between Birmingham and London, the G.W.R. line from Oxford to London already being in use.

Plate 12        Olton Reservoir showing a boat house & the Keepers cottage.

The coming of the railway brought about a gradual decline in the prosperity of canals over the next 50 years as freight which the canals had transported between cities was transferred to the railways.

The Tithe map indicates the type of agriculture in all parts of the parish of Bickenhill. It is clear the main crop must have been corn with 51% of the entire area under arable cultivation. Warwickshire was at that time a 'corn county'. Of the remaining land 35% served as pasture or meadow. There were some market gardens (this form of growing was to increase considerably in the next 100 years in Olton) and a few gravel pits.

The Lyndon Quarter is shown divided between 13 large landowners and some smallholdings, mainly in the northern end of the parish. With the exception of Elizabeth Lee these larger landowners were not farming the land themselves; they are shown to be in the occupation of tenant farmers.

It is interesting to note how scattered the dwellings were, there being no sign of a village community, except for some small groups of cottages at Brook Lane and Ulverley Terrace. Despite some urbanisation during the latter part of the Victorian era this rural scene was to continue well into the 20th. century (Plate 13)

Plate 13                         Haymaking in Olton circa 1885.

From 1860 — 1870 the railways produced a change in the living habits of the middle class. Until then a suburban house had been the privilege of a few well-to-do owners of a carriage and pair. Now the number and frequency of trains allowed any prosperous man to live in a comfortable country home far from work and the noise and dirt of the city.

One of the major factors which led to the development of Olton was the opening of Olton Station in 1864. The other factor was land owner-ship.

The 1839 Tithe map shows only the lower section of St Bernard's Road (Grange Road to Streetsbrook Road). A triangle of land above this road, with the reservoir on the right and Kineton Green Road on the left reaching up as far as the Turnpike road is of interest in Olton's Victorian development. In 1839 this land was divided between five land-owners but by 1869 it was under the ownership of one man, William Williams an Ironmaster from Handsworth. He does not appear to have resided in the area so it may be assumed that he had been buying up parcels of land ready for development when the railway was completed and Olton Station was opened.

Why did he choose Olton for such speculative buying and not land near other proposed stations? This may be explained by the fact that his wife was Anne Tarleton Williams and she was probably related to Richard Tarleton who owned land in the area of Lincoln Road and there-fore William Williams may have had knowledge of the area and the land-owners. Some of the earliest houses in the newly emerging Olton were in Lincoln Road and along the Warwick Road.

James Kent, who was later nicknamed "The King of Olton", appears to have owned land around Bickenhill Hall where he lived in 1871, and he was leasing quite substantial amounts of land from the Josiah Mason Trust in Warwick Road. It was on this land and land owned by William Williams that the Victorian development that now forms Olton's Conser-vation area began.

After the death of William Williams his Trustees decided to sell the land. The first sale of part of the Olton Estate was at the "Hen & Chicken" public house in Birmingham in June 1869. The notice of sale states "A road has recently been constructed through the estate from the Turnpike road and lots of commanding views of Olton Reservoir have been laid out, of various areas, to meet the requirements of parties wishing to erect Villa residences either for their own occupation or for invest-ment".

The plots of land varied in size from 2 acres to 70 acres (Vales Farm) the majority being about 4 acres. Some land was purchased and later divided into smaller plots before being resold. Some purchasers built a house for themselves and other houses which they let to tenants. An example of this can be seen when at the second sale in 1872 Edward Meredith Evans bought Lot 2, a plot of 7 acres. He built and lived in a large detached house with a beautiful garden and orchard stretching to the Reservoir — The Oaklands (No. 42 St Bernard's Road). Over the next 20 years he built houses on the remaining land (Nos. 26—40 St Bernard's Road) which he let to tenants until they were sold, after his death, in 1918.

A covenant was placed on the land at the time of the sale which meant that only those of a certain income level would be able to live on the Olton estate. Only private dwelling houses were to be built and these to be of a value not less than £500, which was a great deal of money in 1869. The result seems to be that the area attracted a reputation of being "special". Research suggests that this reputation was encouraged by some of those who came to live in St Bernard's Road.

One of the first buildings to be erected was the building now known as The Friary. (Plate 14). The land had been offered for sale as Lot 21, "42 acres of land and a commodious farm" called at that time "Folly Hall".

Plate 14          St. Bernard's Monastery at the end of the 19th century.

The land, house and farm were purchased by Bishop Bernard Ullathorne the first Catholic Bishop of Birmingham. Bishop Ullathorne wanted to provide accommodation for the education and training of future priests. Plans for a building were drawn up by Dunn & Hanson, though the original plans were never completely carried out. The building, named in honour of its founder, was ready for occupation in 1873.

The house and farm had become known as St Bernard's Grange and the White's Directory of 1874 shows the house occupied by Canon Estcourt, the Diocesan Treasurer. In 1881 the house and farm belonged to George Mathews. There are many photographs taken in the 1880's (presumably by George Mathews) and these include scenes of the everyday work of the farm which was managed for Mr Mathews by a farm bailiff. The house is now known as St Bernard's Grange and can still be seen near the corner of Grange Road (once known as Folly Lane (Plate 15)) and St Bernard's Road, but there is little evidence of Folly Farm.

In 1889 the Seminary closed and the property came onto the market. At that time the Capuchin Friars were looking for suitable premises and so it became the Franciscan Monastery of the Immaculate Conception.

Plate 15                    Folly Lane (now Grange Road).

A wide corridor, the ambulacrum, overlooking the garden served as a church for parishioners until 1929 when a church, designed by Bernard Cox, was opened.

Enclosed by farmland the Monastery was to change very little over the years, lit only by oil lamps until 1909 when they changed to gas. There was no electricity until 1931. Set back from the road behind the church this handsome red brick building with its many dormer windows retains its peaceful quality to this day.

By 1880 the area was known as Bickenhill Park and considered "a very improving neighbourhood". With 26 daily trains to carry the business man to and from the city whilst his family could enjoy the environment "proverbial for the health'" it soon became a fashionable Victorian residential area.

The Kelly's Directory of 1880 noted "Olton is completely separated from the main parish of Bickenhill; since the greater part of its increasing population dwell about 5 miles from the parish church, it is proposed to constitute a separate parish, and a church called St Margaret's is being erected". (Plate 16)

A committee of 15 chaired by the Rev. Capel, Vicar of Bickenhill, made regular appeals for subscriptions to see St Margaret's firmly established. The first incumbent was to be Arthur Butler, curate of St Mary's, Acocks Green.

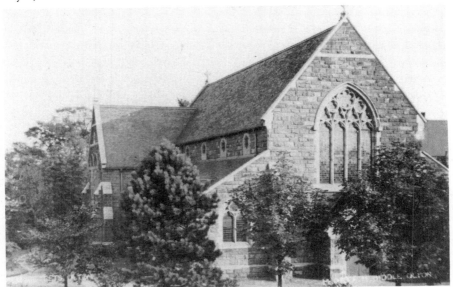

St. Margaret's Church, West Front before the installation of
Plate 16                              the Memorial window — circa 1914.

The land on which the church was built was offered by the representatives of the late William Williams and Mr James Kent. Mr Kent was leasing this land from the Josiah Mason Trust and Rev Butler liked to tell the story of how he "persuaded" Mr Kent to release a piece of land for the church whilst they were travelling by train to Birmingham.

Mr Kent was to be a considerable benefactor to the new parish; in 1887 he also supplied one of his houses as a parsonage. (Now the doctors surgery in St Margaret's Road).

Rev Butler worked tirelessly to raise funds envisaging a grand parish church with a tower and a spire. Plans were submitted by the architect J.G. Bland but tenders were "so much in excess of that we expected and of our present funds" that a portion of the church only was built by Bromwich & Foster of Rugby. The foundation stone had been laid by Mrs Evans, wife of the Rector of Solihull. Under the stone they buried a bottle containing four newspapers of the day and coins of silver from 1d. to 2/6d. dated 1879.

Fund raising continued since it soon became clear that the church was not big enough, there being an absence of adequate free seating accommodation. Rev Butler felt that as there were only 18 free seats for some 200 children, 400 cottagers and 80 servants, this discouraged regular church attendance. Those who were able to afford it rented a pew and this was one of the most important sources of income for the new church.

As funds became available a local architect, Benjamin Corser, was appointed to design the extensions for the church. The foundation stone for the Nave and Transepts was laid by the Countess of Warwick in 1895. On 10th March 1896 the Bishop of Worcester came for the re-opening of the enlarged church and thanks to many generous donations, Dr Butler was able to note "the interior will be more finished and beautiful than I ever anticipated".

Soon Dr Butler's mind was fixed upon the idea of a parish school and he set about raising the money with the same zeal as he had for the church. The site for St Margaret's School in Richmond Road was purchased for £230 and the foundation stone was laid on 26th May 1883. The building, designed by Benjamin Corser, cost £685 and was first used as a day school in January 1885. In the parish magazine Rev Butler encourages the children "to be regular in attendance to take advantage of the most thorough Elementary Education".

The material needs of his parishioners were also important to Dr Butler; he had special concern for those less fortunate in his flock. The Medical & Clothing Club was formed in 1881 to encourage thrift, a family payment of 1½d. a week ensuring medical attention and medicines. He was saddened by the "distress in consequence of want of work" and sought to provide "wholesome recreation" at the working mens' club with cricket and football and urged them to improve their gardens to provide extra food for the family.

After the death of Mrs Hasluck of Olton Court in 1901 the family presented her Mission room to the parish. For a time no suitable place could be found for it and then in 1904 Mr Ward gave some land in Warwick Road where the Mission room was rebuilt and became known as the Church room. It continued to be the home of many parish groups and can be identified now as the site of a small garden centre near to Mason's Way.

Rev Butler died in 1922 aged 76 having been Vicar of Olton for forty years. A distinctive figure in a frock coat with an imposing beard he was "mainly instrumental in building the church and worked unceasingly for its embellishment and for the provision of schools and a vicarage".

The urbanisation of Olton began in the 1870's and 1880's. St Bernard's Road has been used to illustrate this Victorian scene because by the end of the 19th century most of the houses between Warwick Road and the West Warwickshire cricket ground had been built giving a street picture of mixed but typically Victorian domestic architecture that has changed little since that time.

Although there was considerable building on the Warwick Road and Old Warwick Road it is not as easy to identify the pattern of community life that can be seen in St Bernard's Road. Kineton Green Road did not develop until the early 20th century.

This description of late Victorian life in Olton is inevitably based on a mixture of specific facts and more general knowledge of Victorian times.

The southern end of St Bernard's Road — from Streetsbrook Road to Grange Road — is shown on the 1839 Tithe map. A new road cutting across the fields was constructed in 1869 linking this old road to the Warwick Road opposite to Olton Station. Named Windmill Road it must have been an imposing sight as the houses, set in large gardens on a ridge of land above the surrounding rural countryside, began to be built. (Plate 17). By 1872 this road was named St Bernard's Road taking its name from the seminary built that year.

St. Bernard's Rd, east side. No. 2 was demolished when Warwick Road was widened.

Plate 17

The first house constructed is thought to have been Elmhurst (No.21) which was owned by Dr John Thomas, the founder of the Christadelphians, though he never lived there. The house was however used for a Fraternal Gathering in 1872 when a huge marquee housed the 200 people who came by train to "Dr Thomas's lonely house".

Other early houses were The Ferns (No. 44), The Oaklands (No. 42) and Oak House which was demolished in 1977. (Hawkeswell Close now occupies the site of Oak House and its garden). It had once been the home of Charles and Caroline Elton who were retired publicans. After her husband's death Caroline built houses for her four children George, John, Caroline and Clara (Numbers 23—29). No. 25 St Bernard's Road — Fairview — was to become the home of Frederick William Lanchester from 1893—1897. Lanchester is remembered as an engineer who, though he had neither craftsmens training nor academic qualifications, worked out new and original designs that resulted in the first full sized British petrol motor car. (Life of an Engineer by Dr. Kinsford)

Lanchester came to Birmingham to work for T.B. Barker a maker of gas engines. He was joined later by his brothers George and Frank and together they set up house in Olton which they furnished from a legacy left by an Aunt. They were looked after by an old family servant who had nursed the boys in infancy. Lanchester had a reputation for careless dress, though never shabby, and could be seen striding around Olton with his coat buttoned in the wrong holes and his trousers baggy at the knees.

Lanchester was interested in the idea of flight and tested gliders from the first floor window of Fairview across the garden to the meadows beyond. He was keen on yachting, a pastime his friend, Dr Bostock Hill had introduced him to some years before. No doubt this interest encouraged him to build a motor boat which was constructed in the back garden and tested on Olton Mere. The boat was launched at Oxford and was still working regularly 40 years later.

As the brothers were free only to work on Frederick's ideas on Sunday, which shocked the good people of Olton, they became known as the "Unholy Trinity". (Life of an Engineer - Kinsford)

Five Victorian houses have been demolished, No. 2 Hillside, removed when the Warwick Road was widened, Oak House, and a group of three houses Viola Cottage, Wychmont and Mereside. Mereside left a plot of land which became Mereside Estate. It was the largest of these houses and is remembered by many as the site of the parish fete for many years. In 1880 it was the home of a merchant named Thomas Richards, his wife and six children. He had a living-in staff of five including a governess, Matilda Lampard from San Francisco. In 1899 the house was owned by

Thomas Walker, an Auctioneer, who took great pride in his garden and its many fine trees. He was said to have been found up in a tree sawing off a dead branch when he was very advanced in years. The garden was extensive reaching as far as the Mere, which his son Maurice would swim across and back before breakfast each day. The grounds also contained a tennis lawn and bowling green about which Mr Walker was most particular.

Mereside was built "side on" to the road as were The Briars (No.69) and The Beeches (No. 73). A strip of land was left between these two houses and it seems that it was used as a narrow lane to Kineton Green.

Plate 18                                  The Beech tree in St. Bernard's Road.

Both houses would have faced onto this lane. A portion of this lane remains as Chestnut Close. The Beeches was well named for its garden at one time contained some fine beech trees one of which stood, literally, in the road for many years. Described as one of the most beautiful sights in Olton, it was cut down about twelve years ago as it was said to cause a hazard to traffic.(Plate 18). Evidence of the many fine gardens can be seen in the large number and variety of trees still remaining, and in those much loved Victorian hedges of Holly, Laurel and Privet. Photographs do survive of Wychmont showing a balustraded terrace above lawns on three levels sweeping down to the Mere, and of The Spinney (No. 74) taken in 1914 at the double wedding of Mr Terry's stepdaughters Florence and Charlotte. The guests (including Rev Butler) were entertained in a garden pretty with trellis roses and neat flower beds.

The houses in St Bernard's Road have, with one or two exceptions, changed very little in the last 100 years. It is still possible to walk along the road and appreciate their qualities and it is not difficult to imagine them at the turn of the century. Along a one mile stretch are a wide range of architectural styles. Some reflect the Georgian influence such as No. 52, others Victorian Gothic like No. 62, whilst later houses such as No. 74 show the Voysey influence of the early 20th century. Only two architects have been identified as having designed more than two houses in St Bernard's Road. One was John Osborne who designed Nos. 26, 80 and 105. Osborne was also the architect of the Congregational Church in Kineton Green Road. The other was Benjamin Corser (Plate 19)

Plate 19                    Benjamin Corser, Architect, and his wife.

who lived at 54, St Bernard's Road from 1884 until his death in 1919. He was married to Frances, the youngest daughter of Zaccheus Walker of Fox Hollies Hall, Birmingham. Corser was the architect chosen when St Margaret's Church was enlarged. He also had considerable influence on its interior, being the designer of the reredos which was built in 1901 and occupies the whole width of the chancel. The choir stalls and altar rail built in 1904 and the alabaster font and oak litany desk made in 1913 are further examples of Corser's work. In 1898 James Grice, a neighbour, employed Corser to design three houses for him in St Bernard's Road. They were called Greenhill, Rosehill and Falconhill (Nos. 15, 17 and 19). He was also the architect of St Margaret's School, now demolished, which occupied a site in Richmond Road close to the canal.

Some of Benjamin Corser's other work includes Water Orton Church, Dudley Art School and Free Library and Birmingham Athletic Institute.

One of the largest houses in St Bernard's Road and the least obvious to passers-by, is Olton Court (No. 89) St Bernard's Road). (Plate 20). The land on which it was built was purchased in 1872 by Daniel Hasluck, the site was over 12 acres of fields and woods. The house was built in 1895 and enlarged in 1899.

Mrs Hasluck was a generous benefactor to St Margaret's Church, her name appears on most donation lists for the church building and its contents. In 1895 she gave two windows in memory of her husband

Plate 20                                                    Olton Court circa 1903.

and parents.   She clearly put considerable time into good works running a Mission room at Kineton Green which became a well attended feature of the area with Mothers meetings, Bible class and a sewing club "for adult cottagers and servants wishing to make profitable use of a Sunday afternoon".

When Mrs Hasluck died suddenly in Llandudno in 1901 Dr Butler wrote "her loss seems irreparable — she was as good as a curate to me in the very practical assistance she so liberally gave".

After Mrs Hasluck's death Olton Court was purchased by the Sisters of Our Lady of Compassion.   Some of the land was sold separately and the houses built on this land are Nos. 103—109 St Bernard's Road.

The Sisters came from France in 1903.   They arrived at Olton Station on a particularly wet and stormy night and were helped to the Convent by a resident of St Bernard's Road who supplied a buggy to transport their trunks.

The grounds of the Convent were still extensive going through to Kineton Green Road;   they included a small wooded area (where the Servite flats now stand) and an orchard containing apple, plum and damson trees.   There were also huge glass houses and Sister Claire remembers these as "looking like a lake when the sun shone on the glass". Beautiful formal gardens surrounded the house.

The Sisters opened a school "for the daughters of gentlemen" and it began with just four pupils.   The school grew to be much respected and at one time had over 70 boarders.   Almost all small children went to the Convent school and many stayed on to complete their education.   The day pupils were a familiar sight walking along St Bernard's Road in their uniform of navy blue trimmed with light and dark blue ribbons.   There was no electricity at the Convent until World War II, one of the Sisters having the daily task of lighting the gas lamps.

Olton Court stands today on a much smaller site yet still retains the peace and tranquility of a bygone age.

With the rapid expansion of 19th century Birmingham as a manufacturing centre there came an increase in the number of prosperous business and professional people.   They had lived in fashionable town squares and rows but by the middle of the century "close population, noxious fumes and the continual smoke arising from the immense quantity of coal consumed" made the well-to-do look for alternative accommodation in one of the "village" suburbs which began to circle the city.

After a long day at work they would take the train away from the noise and dirt of the city to the unspoilt countryside of Olton. They would arrive at a station that had neat flower beds and hanging baskets overflowing with geraniums. (Plate 21). Old photographs confirm that the stationmaster took great pride in the appearance of Olton Station. Cabbies would be waiting, under the bridge if it was wet, to take them to their front door. An oasis of domestic order to which the successful business man could return at the end of the day.

One of the cornerstones of the Victorian Middle classes was work, meaning work outside the home as domestic work of any kind was for servants. In a large percentage of those families living in St Bernard's Road at the end of the century the head of the household had his own business and they represented a wide range of trades and professions.

There were several from the jewellery trade, John Middleton, a silversmith, lived at Stratford House (No. 49) from 1880 until his death in 1907. He was one of the founders and a deacon of the Congregational Church in Kineton Green Road which bears a plaque to his memory.

Two gun makers are known to have lived in St Bernard's Road. James Scott of Rowanleigh (No. 37) who became the President of Olton Cricket Club and William Powell who was head of the well known gun

Plate 21    Olton signal box with every available space filled with flowers.

making firm in Carr's Lane dating back to 1802. For 40 years William Powell was the guardian of the Birmingham gun barrel proof house and for a considerable term its Honorary Treasurer. (Plate 22). He did a great

Plate 22    William Powell, Gunmaker and Guardian of the Birmingham Gun Barrel Proof House until 1901.

deal to enhance the reputation of Birmingham work and took great pride in the craft of gun making.    He lived at Lyndhurst (No. 33) until his death aged 83 in 1905, he is buried in the Friary cemetery.

There were manufacturers of a wide range of goods from tubes to safety lamps and cycle saddles to steel pens.    Joseph Cooke of Oakleigh (No. 88) was Birmingham's first producer of the Davy safety lamp. (Plates 23 A&B)   Edward Lycett, who lived at Eastwood (No.59) from 1895 until 1904 when he moved to Oak House, made cycle saddles. Cycling was an increasingly popular pursuit and the Rolls Royce of

Plate 23A                          A lamp from the Catalogue of Joseph Cooke.

Plate 23B.   Joseph Cooke, Safety Lamp Manufacturer.

cycling was a James Bicycle with a Lycett saddle.   Charles Leonardt's
Universal Pen works in Charlotte Street manufactured high quality steel
pens which were exported to Europe, South America and throughout,
what was then, the British Empire.   He lived at Calonia (No.11) from
1899 to 1904.

There were four doctors who came to live in St Bernard's Road and stayed for many years.    Dr Lunn and Dr Bradford had a surgery at Elvet (No. 1) and Dr Mundy Cox lived at Dodona (No. 12).    At one time these three owned the only cars in Olton.    Dr Lunn and Dr Cox had a single cylinder DeDion.    Dr Bradford made his rounds in a tiller steered Lanchester driven by his chauffeur, both men wearing top hats their long beards blowing in the breeze.    The fourth doctor was Alfred Bostock Hill the Public Analyst for Coventry, Leamington Spa and Stratford.    He lived at Elmhurst (No. 21) from 1888 − 1896 when he moved to Ducie House (No. 62).

In Victorian society the man ruled the house and it was run primarily for his comfort and convenience. He came in from work and expected to find order and peace. He set the rules and was obeyed by the family as well as the servants. It was his wife's responsibility to run the house in an efficient manner. Mrs Beeton wrote "the highest rank of feminine character is knowledge of household duties". This meant organising the work of servants. The census of 1881 shows that in the 19 houses that were then in St Bernard's Road there were 31 servants living in. Employing domestic staff was a sign of social status in the 19th. century when the number of people able to afford servants rose sharply. By 1900 domestic work was the major employer of women. Most of those described in the census are general servants — the maids of all work — many very young. Thirteen were aged between 15 and 19 years. They were given a sparsely

Plate 24

Victorian servants in their black afternoon frock and lace trimmed aprons.

furnished attic room and two working outfits. A cotton dress in pink, blue or lilac worn with a plain white cap and apron and an afternoon dress in black with a frilled cap and lace trimmed apron. (Plate 24) Most houses list only one living in servant and with all there was to do in these large houses they must have worked very hard for long hours. Mrs Beeton wrote. . . . "A general servant's duties are so multifarious that unless she be quick and active she will not be able to accomplish all". In addition most houses had daily help from laundresses, sewing maids, cooks, gardeners, carriage drivers and later chauffeurs and motor mechanics.

When not involved with domestic life the ladies gave much of their time to worthy causes. Rev Butler often remarks in the parish magazine about the good work done to raise money for the church and church school and "the efforts of lady visitors in befriending our cottagers".

Many stories are told that people who came to live in St Bernard's Road made a conscious effort to remain separate from the rest of the developing community in Olton. One story tells that you were discouraged from walking along the road unless you lived there. If this is true it helps to confirm the view that the road was a community within itself having schools, shops and churches close by.

They provided their own social life with concerts and magic lantern shows and in the winter there was skating on the Reservoir. Most winters it seems were cold enough for skating to be a regular pastime. (Plate 25)

Plate 25

Mrs. Mathews, Winnie, Georgie & Mary of St. Bernard's Grange warmly dressed on a frozen Olton Reservoir.

At night people of all ages would gather forming into long chains to skate, each person with a candle lit chinese lantern. In the summer many gardens were the setting for tennis or croquet parties and many a courtship blossomed as boy met girl under Mama's watchful eye.

Another important social occasion was being "at home". Everyone had a certain time when it was known they would be at home to callers. The house received a special clean and polish and the lady receiving guests put on her best tea gown. Tiny sandwiches and attractive cakes were laid out with the best tea service to await the arrival of visitors. If you called at the wrong time you left your card on a salver on the hall table. The leaving and returning of cards was an important social ritual that was to continue, to a lesser degree, in St Bernard's Road until the late 1930's.

The weekends were the only time the whole family had together, Saturday would be spent cycling or taking a carriage ride into the local countryside. Later with the coming of the motor car there were family outings to Stratford-Upon-Avon or Warwick.

Before the turn of the century several sports clubs had been set up in the vicinity of St Bernard's Road. The first to be formed was Olton Cricket Club in 1888. The early activities of the cricket club are detailed in the parish magazine of the day. Clearly Rev Butler was a lover of cricket and he seems to have been instrumental in the club's formation. The first President was James Kent and he also provided the grounds. How often Mr Kent provided the land for one of Rev Butler's projects! It is not recorded where this ground was but by 1890 new grounds had been acquired from Mr Richards.

In 1897 the President was James Scott of Rowanleigh (No.37) and of the 38 committee members, 28 were residents of St Bernard's Road. During that year ownership of the field had been acquired by Olton Grounds Limited, and Rev Butler stated in the parish magazine "The body purchased the land in the interest of sport and recreation generally and moreover consisting as it does, of gentlemen who are connected with, and have the welfare of the Olton Cricket Club at heart the movement will be hailed with universal satisfaction". (The ground is still owned in this way). The club went from strength to strength its grounds at one time described as "second to none, with the exception of the county ground". The annual match with Warwickshire was always a great event with players such as Santall, Lilley and Willie Quaife delighting the spectators with their skills.

Olton Hockey Club had been formed in 1898 by two Solihull School teachers, J.F. Brown and D.H. English, and it produced many players who were to represent Warwickshire (including Willie Quaife (Fig.26) see part

Plate 26

Olton Hockey team 1910 — William Quaife standing 2nd from the right.

III). The Ladies section was formed in 1913, at that time they played on a pitch at Olton Convent. They joined the Mens' Hockey Club in 1914.

Robin Hood Golf Club was formed in 1893. It began as a nine hole course on land between Lakey Lane and Stratford Road rented for £5 per year with a membership of 25 gentlemen. Many of the early members were residents of Birmingham and the club provided transport to the course from Acocks Green Station. One of these early members was Dr Frank Stableford the inventor of the golf scoring system which bears his name.

Olton Golf Club began in the same year. It grew from the enthusiasm of J.P. Heaton who lived at Doehurst(No. 26 St. Bernards Road) from 1890. Mr Heaton had become interested in golf and decided to have his own nine hole course constructed so that he might pursue this new found interest. (His name appears as a possible member of Robin Hood Golf Club and there is no explanation as to why he decided to lay out his own course rather than take up this membership).

Friends expressed interest in his plans and Olton Golf Club was born in November 1893 with Mr Heaton as Honorary Secretary. In 1895 the course was extended to 18 holes and in 1903 the club leased Olton House as a club house. (This building, now demolished, was at one time known as Price's Farm).

Mr Heaton was a keen sportsman having been both athlete and cricketer. His name appears along with George Godfrey and Harry Harthill in the early records of most of the sports clubs that were formed at the end of the last century. Their enthusiasm for sport has left Olton with facilities for golf, cricket, hockey, fishing and sailing.

Five residents of St Bernard's Road became the first lessees of Olton Reservoir from the Canal Company. They all lived in houses which overlooked the Reservoir and no doubt had direct access from their gardens. One of them John Florence, an Auctioneer, who lived at Wychmont (now demolished) was a keen angler. An Honorary Treasurer of the Birmingham & Midland Counties Piscatorial Association it was he who laid down the original rules for fishing. The club formed in 1900 by the lessees and ten subscribers with the privilege of sailing, fishing and shooting. Shooting was suspended in 1926 owing to a shortage of wildfowl although an occasional shoot took place when rabbits became a problem in neighbouring gardens. Local people still refer to the bunny fields or Bunny Lane (Grange Road). Mark Mintram was the first keeper employed by the club which he served for more than 40 years. (Plate 27) He lived beside the reservoir in a small cottage which also served as a club house for members.

Plate 27

Mark Mintram keeper of the Reservoir for 40 years and his wife Anne.

70

Walks were a popular family activity.   Miss Margaret Pedley who lived at Greenhill (No.17) in the early years of this century wrote that "we would turn off Kineton Lane at the little triangular green past an old farm on the right, down to the Brook with its footbridge and on up into Gospel Lane.   It was a real lane, with fields and trees on either side. At the end, just before we came out onto the Warwick Road there was a Georgian Farmhouse and from there we could walk back along the Hollow.   Our favourite walk was along Grange Road, my two brothers would hang over the bridge to watch the trains go by.   I knew all about 'saddle tanks' and two cylinder 4—6—2's.   What a great thrill it was to see Katerfelto or one of that class.   We would complete the walk by going past Dove House Farm — half timbered and very beautiful and down Ulverley Green Road".

On Sundays people would be seen in their best clothes making their way to church, afterwards they would "walk the road" meeting friends and neighbours to talk for a while before returning to Sunday lunch. This always consisted of a joint of beef, lamb or mutton and when the meal was over and cleared away the afternoon would be spent reading, for entertainment, even for the children, was not encouraged on the Sabbath.

Shopkeepers came to supply the needs of this expanding community. Orders were collected by tradesmen or taken to the shop by a servant. Once the order was made up it would be delivered to the house, trades-

Plate 28        Olton Post Office 1902 looking towards Ulverley Green Road.

71

Plate 29    Warwick Rd/Lincoln Rd junction 1902, only the cottage on the right remains today.   The two figures stand at what is now a busy roundabout.

men showed their appreciation of the custom they received and would often include a "little something extra" with the order, especially at Christmas time.

On the corner of Warwick Road and Ulverley Green Road was the Post office. (Plate 28)   The original shop was wedge shaped and looked like a Toll House.   As well as being the Post Office it became a general grocers.    Stamps and parcels were dealt with on the right hand side, while to the left and at the back of the shop they sold all manner of groceries.    Of particular delight to the children were the large slabs of toffee and chocolate that were broken up and sold in two penny bars.

By the end of the 19th century there was an increasing demand for houses close to the "village" of Olton.    Indeed the development can be seen to radiate outwards, albeit in small pockets, from the area close to Olton Station with building in Richmond Road, Ulverley Green Road, Lincoln Road, Lyndon Road and Castle Lane.(Plate 29)

These more modest villas or terraces were in sharp contrast to the large houses with extensive gardens that had been built when Bickenhill Park began some 30 years before.   They indicate a different population and a different reason for growth, supplying staff for the large houses, gardeners, coachmen etc. and workers for the market gardens and farms.

Despite these changes Olton was to remain a largely rural area for the next 40 years as development was mostly confined to land that had been owned by William Williams and the land controlled by James Kent.

# CHANGING SCENES & FAMOUS PEOPLE

Gowan Bank *1920*

*by Carol Andrews*

This continuation of the History of Olton concentrates mainly on the late Victorian and early Twentieth Century development of the area. It is, as far as possible, historically accurate, yet at the same time enriched with memories related to me by countless senior citizens of Olton. To these warm and friendly people I would like to say a very big and sincere, "thank you". The historical facts herein are like a black and white photograph: the memories give us colour.

My aim has been to paint a picture with words, so that you, my reader, may walk, in imagination, through the streets and lanes of Olton, around the turn of the Century, and know some of its characters.

The story opens with one of the richest and most powerful men in Olton's Victorian past; James Kent.

"Gowan Bank"
Olton. 1986

James Kent was one of the most influential figures in the Victorian development of Olton. He was a boot and shoemaker with premises in Snow Hill, Birmingham, being a wealthy businessman and bachelor, shown on the 1871 Census as living at Bickenhill Hall, Olton.

In 1873 he leased from the Josiah Mason Trust, "The Chapel Field Estate" which included a sixteenth century farmhouse, known as "Chapel Fields Farm", and a little more than ninety six acres of land, mostly north of the Warwick Road, in Olton. He was obliged to pay a yearly rent of £300 to the Trust for the first three-years of his tenancy and thereafter £450 per annum with a lease of one hundred and twenty years.

James Kent was advised by the Josiah Mason Trust to, "lay out these lands in a suitable and proper manner", to form roads and streets, and told that he must then erect villa residences and dwellinghouses, some of which were to bring in a yearly rent of £30 and others of £20. The Trust demanded that, in the first five years of his lease, Mr Kent must spend £4,000 and in the subsequent six years a similar sum, and he was to provide receipts as proof of his expenditure.

James Kent did not set up a new system of roads. He merely extended Richmond Road into Richmond Park and Lyndon Road, in which he built quite a lot of houses, was not improved until 1904, a year after his death. Prior to this it had been a narrow country lane in parts with high banks on either side. (Plate 30)

The Josiah Mason Trust largely dictated the types of housing that James Kent was to build. The middle class residences that appeared along the Warwick Road from the corner of Richmond Road, down into Olton Hollow, were designed to bring in a higher rent than the smaller houses in Richmond Road and Lyndon Road. Many of the houses on the Warwick Road incorporated expensive fittings, including ornate stained glass front doors.

Shops for Oltons increasing population were now desirable, so Mr Kent built a row along the Warwick Road in Olton Hollow in 1883. He inserted a stone plaque in the wall above them which read, egotistically, "Kentish New Town". Even the roofing tiles were stamped, "J. Kent".

Rows of dwellings gradually appeared along Richmond Road in the late 19th century destined to be homes for workers in the lower income bracket. (Plate 31) All the houses were alike, and built in terraces. The tenants were required to pay a weekly rental of seven shillings and six pence (37.5p). Each house had six rooms, a kitchen and scullery, as well

Plate 30                                Lyndon Road before alterations.

Plate 31                    Houses in Richmond Park 1900 (now Richmond Rd).

          The Lodge, Richmond Rd circa 1900.   The gates were the entrance
Plate 32                                            to Richmond Park.

as a long garden.  Rates were £5 per annum for the tenants, who had very little in the way of modern amenities.  There was no mains water, no electricity or gas and no road lighting, or made-up pavements.  Sanitation was very primitive — and probably consisted of an outside earth or bucket closet.

The Lodge, (Plate 32) now number 49 Richmond Road remains something of a mystery.  It would appear that it was designed as a lodge for a big house that was subsequently built elsewhere. This house could have been Bickenhill Hall. (See page 89 Chapter 12).    Interestingly, recent excavations in the Lodge garden have revealed some shoe lasts, which could suggest a connection with James Kent.

Just below the Station, high on the embankment in Richmond Road, Kent built a row of five cottages.  The end house, number five, was Mrs Greensill's shop, the first to open in Richmond Road. (Plate 33) One of the early cottage residents was Herbert Stowell, the Congregational Minister, who lived at Number one for a while before moving to a bigger house that Kent had built on the Warwick Road.

James Kent was now landlord to a vast number of tenants, and had employed his old friend William Ward to be his bailiff.   The baptismal register at St Margaret's Church records the christening, in 1891, of

Plate 33            Cottages beside the railway bridge in Richmond Rd. 1903.

"Baron Kent Ward", William's only son, and Kent's Godson. At the time Kent prophesied that, one day, his new Godson would be very wealthy.

In fact fate took a hand in this forecast, for although William Ward was the sole beneficiary of Kent's estate when he died in 1903, it was Helen Ward, William's daughter, who eventually became leasee of the Josiah Mason Trust land. William Ward died on March 1st 1938, whilst living at "Sutton Grange", Solihull. James Kent's grave can be found in St Mary's Churchyard, Acocks Green. A newspaper report of his death records the fact that local people had nick-named him, "The King of Olton", and so, to many, he must have appeared.

As some of the photographs in this book illustrate, there were numerous farms in Olton at the turn of the century. Most of the farm-houses have been demolished in the urban development of the area, including Chapel Fields Farm, mentioned in the previous chapter.

The name "Chapel Fields" is derived from the fact that it stood on, or near, the site of the Chapel known to have been standing in 1350, of the former Parish of Lyndon. The farmhouse was a 16th or early 17th Century building, with timber framed wattle and daub walls. An addition to the left-hand side of the main building was probably added in the 19th Century. The 1834 first edition Ordnance Survey Map of Lichfield and Birmingham marks Chapel Fields Farm as being just off the southerly end of Lyndon Road.

Among the best features of the house were the two ornate tall brick chimneys that can be seen in the photograph below. (Plate 34) The interior boasted an impressive banqueting room, into which, many Olton-ians were invited to celebrate 'D' Day in 1944. On this occasion,

Plate 34                                    Chapelfields Farm circa 1900.

numerous children explored the secret passages, that were hidden behind the farmhouse kitchen walls.

Olton has lost comparatively few of its beautiful buildings, but the demolition of Chapel Fields Farmhouse in 1954 is perhaps the saddest destruction in the area.

Two farmhouses that have survived however, are "Dovehouse" and "Ulleries Farm". "Dovehouse Farm", in Dovehouse Lane, is Olton's only listed building to date. It was part of the former Elmdon Hall Estate and is described in the 1920/30 Sale Catalogue of the Estate as a "picturesque homestead", with porch entrance, two large sitting rooms with casement windows, kitchen with double range, scullery, dairy, and six bedrooms". In its bricked yard was a soft water tank, well and pump. The building dates from around 1500, and was tenanted by Edmund Lea for many years in the early part of the present century. Many Oltonians still call it "Leas Farm". Mr Lea had a large Dairy herd and sold milk to many local customers, to whom he delivered twice daily. His hens had a reputation for laying astray, and children could often be seen searching the surrounding lands in hopes of an egg for tea.

Another farm in the Elmdon Hall Estate within the Olton area was "Ulverley Hall Farm", near Olton Station, which only had 43 acres and was tenanted by Mrs Caddick.

Ulleries Farm (Plate 35) now number 138 Lyndon Road is a modest but attractive early 19th. century building. The resident farmer from the turn of this century until 1932 was Mr Beamon. The Beamons were staunch Methodists, Mrs Beamon being a familiar figure who always wore black or dark grey, usually a long skirt and high necked blouse, with her hair done in a tight bun at the nape of her neck. They had one son called Billy. The farm land stretched from below the present shops in Lyndon Road, to the current Barrington Road area, and back almost to Lode Lane. It had nearly one hundred acres, and was thus larger than Chapel Fields Farm prior to 1873. However the Ulleries Farm land was gradually sold off in the urbanisation of Olton. Firstly the George Vth Jubilee Park was opened on its land, and then Ulleries Road was built just before World War II. The road was named after the farm, which is shown on the first Lichfield and Birmingham Ordnance Survey Map of 1834, as "Hullery" or "Ulverley".

Mr Beamon specialised in Dairy Farming. The cows were shorthorn, mostly red roan, as were many of the cows in Olton at that time. Mangel-wurzels were grown as cattle food in the fields that bordered Lyndon Road. There was a farm worker, known as a "waggoner", called Mr Dodd who smoked a clay pipe, which often broke, but he always seemed to have a spare one in his pocket.

Plate 35     The Beamon family outside Ulleries Farm in Lyndon Rd 1904.

Plate 36          Women Haymaking near St. Bernard's Grange circa 1885.

Haymaking at the turn of the Century was a very time and labour consuming occupation.. (Plate 36) Community spirit was high, and people who had no connection with farming for the rest of the year, often helped to harvest the hay and grain crops.   Many Olton hands did indeed make light work.   There were rides in the wagons for children, and lavish home-made teas, with bread, butter, jams and cakes.   The large open spaces and fields were a haven for children, who sometimes occupied themselves by damming up Hatchford Brook to make a bathing pool.   Irate farmers, their cattle starved of water, after a vain chase of the children, would break down the dam, but the proceedure was invariably repeated the next day.

Rural Olton was undeniably beautiful and those who remember it are fortunate indeed.   However, thanks to Edith Holden's "Nature Notes" of 1906, published in the form of "The Country Diary of an Edwardian Lady", people all over the world can share some of the flora and fauna that was abundant in the rich farm-land of the area.

## CHAPTER 11

# *THE ORIGINS OF CONGREGATIONAL WORSHIP IN OLTON*

Congregational witness in Olton is thought to have begun in about 1820, when the Reverend Thomas Hood of Solihull, a great evangelist and teacher, who founded the Congregational Church in Hampton in Arden, is known to have preached at Kineton Green.    He may also have stood under the Gospel Oak tree in Beeches Lane, which in the 1920's became known as Gospel Lane. (Plate 37)  It is understood that fifty years later services were being held in the farmhouse of Ulverley Hall farm, now demolished, which stood at the corner of Ulverley Green Road and Castle Lane.

In 1879 a building which had housed both a butchers shop and a blacksmiths smithy, beside the railway bridge on the Warwick Road, Olton, was purchased by the Congregationalists, with a view to converting it into a Chapel.    New arched windows were inserted, and a small enclosed porch was added onto the front, with a door at either side. (Fig. 38).    Mr Henry Rudge was employed as both Lay Pastor for the services held in the upper part of the building, and teacher for the day school in the basement.

Students from Mansfield College took turns to take the services when Pastor Rudge retired, and Mrs Edgar became the first schoolmistress for the day school.    However, in 1893 the cellar area was found to be unsuitable for a school, and the children, who averaged 34 in number, were transferred to St Margaret Church School in Richmond Road.    In the Spring of 1894, Herbert Stowell, a student from Mansfield College, took the Easter services, and in 1895 he became permanent Pastor at a stipend of £150 per annum.    He married Florence Middleton, the daughter of John Hartshorn Middleton, a silversmith from St Bernard's Road, who was one of the Trustees and early Deacons of the Chapel.

Towards the close of the 19th Century a piece of land at the Northerly end of Kineton Green Road was purchased at a cost of £400 from Daniel Holloway, as a site for a larger Congregational Church.   W.H. Bidlake, one of the foremost Arts and Craft Movement architects, drew up plans for the new building, but the design was thought to be too expensive to erect, and Mr John Osborne's plan was adopted instead.    Mr Thomas Turton built the church which was opened for worship on January 1st, 1901. (Plate 39)

Plate 37        Beeches (later Gospel) Lane from a postcard by Frank Biddle.

Plate 38        Congregational Chapel on the Warwick Road circa 1900.

Plate 39A        Congregational Church Kineton Green Road 1914.

Plate 39B        Harvest at Olton Congregational Church
c 1901–1907.

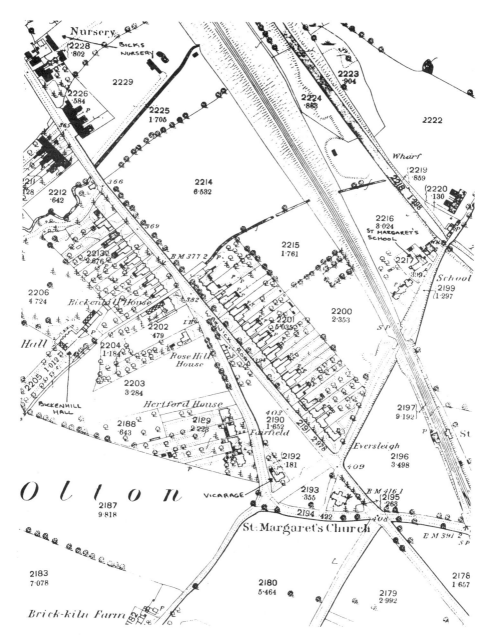

Fig. 8    Reproduced from 1887 O.S. Map showing part of Warwick Road.

87

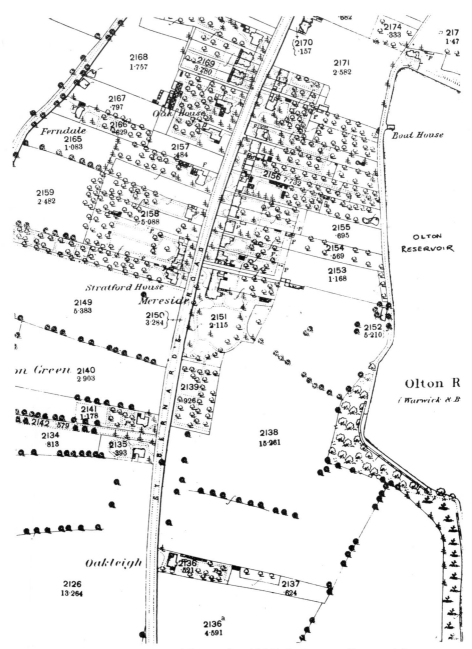

Fig. 7 Reproduced from the 1887 Ordnance Survey Map
showing the North end of St. Bernard's Rd.

Bickenhill Hall was built between the years 1861–1871, when Olton was still in the Parish of Bickenhill. As can be seen from the accompanying Ordnance Survey Map of 1887, the imposing house was set well back from the Warwick Road, and approached along a winding drive lined with trees. (Plate 40) At the Warwick Road entrance gates there was a small lodge for the caretaker.

The first known resident at Bickenhill Hall, as previously mentioned, was James Kent. It is possible that he built the hall as a somewhat grandiose home for himself, and with a view to profit-making, but as the deeds no longer exist, it has not been possible to verify this supposition.

James Kent only lived at the hall for a few years, as by 1881 it was the residence of the Arnold family. David Arnold and his wife had seven children. Their third daughter Lillian, was born in Olton, and later achieved some fame and recognition as a journalist and authoress. Between the years 1903 and 1933 she wrote numerous books, one of which entitled "The Storm Dog" was said, by contemporary critics, to compare favourably with the work of both Hardy and Balzac.

Plate 40                    Bickenhill Hall (Olton College) circa 1899.

Plate 41                              Olton College, staff and girls circa 1917.

In 1899 Bickenhill Hall became a school known as "Olton College for girls".(Plate 41) It also had a Preparatory Class for boys. The school was run by two Welsh sisters, the Misses Balgarnie. The elder of the two, Miss Balgarnie the Principal, was a graduate of London University. She was a keen disciplinarian, and many of the girls were slightly afraid of her. The taller sister, Miss Cox Balgarnie, had a much softer and more kindly disposition. She was a very able musician, and had been trained by a pupil of Sir Charles Halle.

Olton College was seemingly one of the most highly regarded of many private schools that were to be found in Olton at the turn of the century. There were several others along the Warwick Road, including Blenheim Girls Preparatory School run by Emma Lawrence, whose husband, Edmund was a sword cutler. However, Olton College was very much the finishing school for the area, teaching desirable social graces to Middle Class young ladies, and it drew pupils from Hall Green and Acock's Green, as well as from local affluent families. It was set in five acres of ground, and had its own playing fields and tennis lawns. Termly fees for the younger children were three guineas, increasing to four guineas for girls over the age of twelve. The curriculum included all the usual academic subjects, and also Latin which was normal in private boys schools but quite an unusual subject for girls during this period.

In front of the school was a grassy slope, and during the hard winters at the turn of the Century, this was regularly used by the children for toboganning.   In Summer, tennis was a favourite sport and one memorable day one of the girls exclaimed to Miss Cox, "I am so hot I'm sweating!".   "No, no my dear," said Miss Cox aghast, "You must always remember,

> Horses sweat,
>> Gentlemen perspire,
>>> but ladies are all aglow".

Around 1919 Bickenhill Hall ceased to be a school.   The Misses Balgarnie moved back to Wales, to Portmadoc, where they started another private school.   A few of the Olton College girls went with them, to complete their education, as boarders.

In time Bickenhill Hall was divided into flats, and gradually the building degenerated.   The trees grew tall, overhanging the drive, and they became a favourite nesting site for rooks.   Many local people had never seen the Hall which was completely hidden from the road.   In 1932 it was demolished during the urban development of Olton.   At about this time the Lodge, then the home of the Dumbletons, was also demolished, and became the site of Olton Cinema.

The architects of Olton Cinema were Horace G. Bradley and Mr Clarke, and the Olton picture palace was opened around 1934.   It remained until September 1972, when it too was demolished to make way for the present "Virginia House".

# CHAPTER 13: THE DEVELOPMENT OF KINETON GREEN ROAD

Kineton Green Road, in the early Nineteenth Century, was a narrow winding country lane, and pre-dates the North Eastern end of St Bernard's Road. "Kineton Lane" as it was then called, is shown on both the first Ordnance Survey map of 1834, and also the Tithe maps of that era.

The road, in its present form, began developing for housing purposes in the latter half of the Nineteenth Century, with the group of cottages that now exist just south of Chestnut Close. (Plate 42) Local Heresay has, for many years, maintained that the row of cottages on the south-east side of the road (now numbers 121 — 131) were built as farmworkers homes for "Olton Court". As the cottages pre-date Olton Court this cannot be possible. However, it seems likely that they were labourers dwellings for one the many local farms and were built circa 1860.

Along the back of these cottages was a communal right of way for the residents giving access to a row of outside 'privies' or toilets, which flanked the shared wash house, with its double furnace, and sink facilities. These fascinating buildings still exist, and in May 1985 an old "dolly peg" was discovered in the wash house, which is still virtually in its original condition. There was also a communal well for the cottagers.

Plate 42                 Cottages in Kineton Green Road, late 19th century.

On the opposite side of the road is another row of cottages built in the late Nineteenth Century for workers from Gunns Nursery. This was a thriving business which has only closed in the latter half of this century, and the land of which extended from the present siting of "Gunns Way" to the south westerly end of Kineton Green Road at the St Bernard's Road junction.

"Brookfield Nursery", as it was originally called, was started by William Gunn, and is first shown in the Kellys Directories in 1881. As the name implies, Kineton Brook ran across its land, and was doubtless used to irrigate the fast draining sandy soil in the summer months. Kineton Brook was one of the boundaries to the Ancient Manor of Yardley, and was called "Cinctunes Broc". Even in Edwardian times it was still known as "Boundary Brook". (Plates 43 & 50)

By the turn of this century Mrs Gunn was widowed, and her four sons were in charge of the Nursery. A family home was built (now number 152 Kineton Green Road) and the Gunns called it "Kildonan".

The four young men were known by their staff as "Mr Will", who farmed some of the land and specialised in roses; "Mr John", who ran the business and grew the chrysanthemums and sweet peas; "Mr Stuart" whose forte was vegetables, and "Mr Donald" who had a stall selling produce and seed packets in Birmingham Market. Mr John, when he

Plate 43                          Brook Lane early this century.

married, had his own house, which he called "Brookdale" and is now number 75 Kineton Green Road. The Nursery sold fresh salad and tomatoes in summer, and Mr Donald also made up wedding bouquets for many brides in the area, and also wreaths.

A firm friend of the Gunn family was Harry Lauder, the much loved Scottish comedian, who could often be seen walking in the Nurseries, and was of great interest to curious passers by, who would peer over the hedge in hopes of seeing this famous personage!

The first Middle Class residence to be built in Kineton Green Road was "Ferndale" (now number 55) which appears in the 1881 Kellys Directory as being the home of Mr Henry Cox, electroplater and gilder. It stood on a large plot of land that extended into St Bernard's Road, and though the house faced directly, and had access onto Kineton Green Road, Mr Cox gave his address as being St Bernard's Road. Obviously the class distinction between the two roads was very great, and therefore it was much more desirable to have a St Bernard's Road address.

For several years'in the Nineteenth Century "Ferndale" was the only large house in Kineton Green Road, but as the available spaces for Middle Class residences in St Bernard's Road grew fewer, so the development of Kineton Green Road, and its larger houses, began. One of the first people to spot its potential for this was John Jessop.

*John Arthur Jessop*

In 1896, John Arthur Jessop bought from Daniel Holloway, and Edmund King the farmer at Gospel Farm, Beeches (Gospel) Lane, a large plot of land fronting onto the North-Westerly side of Kineton Green Road. At the age of forty-six, Mr Jessop was retiring from his active involvement as a pharmacist at his chemists shop in Acock's Green, and had decided to invest some of his family wealth in land, in Olton.

A year later, he had a good sized house built for his family, with two handsome bays and partially leaded windows on the ground floor, and neo-gothic arched windows upstairs. It had an integral coach house and separate stable block. The family called their elegant new home "Elford" after the Staffordshire village of the same name, from whence they had come some generations back. Now hardly recognisable, the house has modern additions either side of the original building, and is number 84 Kineton Green Road. In later years "Elford" became known as Kineton Grange.

Mr Jessop and his wife Emily Martha had six children whose names were Ted, Wilfred, Winifred, Ethel, Muriel and Frances. (Plate 44) The Jessops employed a living in maid, a 'daily' to clean, a man to pump

94

Plate 44                    The Jessop family in the garden at 'Elford'.

Plate 45                    Kineton Green Road in 1926.

water every evening in the scullery, and 'Saunders' who tended the large garden and tennis court. Milk was delivered twice a day from "Gospel Farm", thus maintaining the link with Edmund King.

In 1898 John Jessop employed Samuel Bridges, a high class builder from Station Road, Acock's Green, to build four more houses on his land, again to the North-Westerly side of Kineton Green Road. Now numbers 96 — 102, these large, well built late Victorian dwellings were called St Dunstan (96), Oakdale (98), Enderleigh (100) and Stoneleigh (102). Probably because Mr Jessop was a Congregationalist, he put a covenant on all four houses, stating that they were not to be used as ale or brew houses, or as taverns. Respectability was all important if the road was to attract a new class of resident.

Thus began the Middle Class development of Kineton Green Road, which could almost be seen to develop in pockets. (Fig.45) More houses were soon built opposite the ones previously mentioned, in a part of the road that is little changed to this day.

John Jessop owned houses on land further down on the other side of Kineton Green Road, as well as in Lincoln Road and later Brook Lane. He is remembered as a tall, kindly gentleman, and a good landlord. The family are pictured on Plate 44 with their friends the Hollidays, who took on the tenancy of Chapelfields Farm after James Kent died. John Jessop and his wife are seated in the centre of the photograph.

*William Quaife*

Between the turn of this century and the First World War there were a variety of Professional, Business-people and Traders living in Kineton Green Road. Unlike St Bernard's Road, where to be "in trade" was frowned upon, Kineton Green Road had been home to a button-maker at "Ivanhoe" (now number 67), a paper-bag manufacturer at "Marston" (number 12), a draper at St Aubins (number 5), a rating officer at "Berriedale" (number 8) and a jeweller at "Beacon View" (number 10).

In 1910 William Quaife the cricketer moved into the road (Fig.46). Born in Newhaven, Sussex in 1872, W.G. Quaife, as he became known, had been introduced to cricket at the age of 4, by his Grandfather. He, and his brother Walter had received their earliest coaching from the Australian Alfred Shaw, thought to have been one of the best tutors in the game of cricket. William was still in his teens when he and Walter, after playing for Sussex for a short time, accepted an offer to play for Warwickshire, an association that was to last more than 30 years for William.

His first appearance was in 1893 and he marked the occasion by making 101 not out. By 1899 he was playing for England and toured Australia in 1901/2 with McClaren's team.

Plate 46    William Quaife, centre front, sitting at the feet of W.G. Grace.

It was with the County that he showed the style that was to make him popular with the crowds. Willie Quaife, as he was affectionately known, was only 5ft.3ins. tall but he developed a style of play to suit his physique. A model right hand bat, a fine cover fielder and a slow leg break bowler he appears to have become more dangerous as he approached the end of his career. In 1926 at the age of 54 he took 82 wickets in a season. In his final game for Warwickshire he made 115 so ending his career as it had begun by making over 100 runs.

After his retirement Quaife was able to concentrate on his business interests but he continued to play cricket for Olton. In a small building beside the canal in Richmond Road, Olton, Willie Quaife ran a school to coach young cricketers. Dick Lilley, the England wicket-keeper, is thought to have been the person who suggested making and selling cricket bats in a small shop attached to the school. It was very successful, and in the days before the First World War, trading as "Quaife and Lilley", they were pioneering a unique bat with six rubber balls embedded into the handle, which made it very pliable and springy.

The little factory in Richmond Road operated before, and after the Great War and many old customers remember the lathes humming away, filling the air with the smell of wood-shavings, and glue bubbling in a pot on a gas ring.    They also made hockey sticks and tennis racquets.    The prize exhibit, that all little boys wanted to see, was the cricket bat, given to Quaife by W.G. Grace, which was displayed in a glass case on the wall.

Willie Quaife lived at "Poynings" (number 173) Kineton Green Road until his death in 1951.    The house, which he had owned from new, was named after a Sussex village.    The Quaife's were members of Olton Congregational Church.

James Kent had built the row of shops in 'Olton Hollow' (Warwick Road) as his "Kentish New Town" in 1883. As the community of Middle and Working Class people in Olton grew, so also did the numbers of shops to serve their needs. (Plate 47) By 1918 there were seventeen of them, as well as a plumber, Bick Brothers Nursery and Sam Hotchkiss the Upholsterer.

Mr Hotchkiss, who had started his business in 1901, was a familiar figure on his bicycle in St Bernard's Road and Kineton Green Road, where he called to collect chairs that were in need of re-upholstery. Very often he would cycle back to his workshop with a chair perched apparently precariously on his head. He also collected rugs and carpets from the big houses, carrying them back in the same fashion, to beat them clean over his wife's long clothes line.

He, and John Wilson the Plumber, had their businesses at the Southerly end of the row of shops, and down a passageway, between them and the other traders was the St Margaret's Church Room. This had originally been Mrs Hasluck's Mission Room, as described on page 54 in Margaret Jordan's work. It was later used on occasions as an overflow classroom for St Margaret's School. The children always enjoyed their visits to the Warwick Road classroom, for it had a large area behind it, in which they could play.

Plate 47　　　　　　　　　　Shops in 'Olton Hollow' — early 20th century.

Beyond the Upholsterer's the shops in 1918 were as follows:—

| | |
|---|---|
| Mrs Bick | Tobacconist |
| Frank Evans | Fruiterer |
| Thomas Williams | Grocer |
| Mrs Mary Williams | Hardware |
| Miss Florrie Neal | Milliner |
| John Bishop | Draper |
| Francis Musham | Beer Retailer |
| Harold Allman | Newsagent and Post Office |
| Ernest Chubb | Baker |
| Amos Holmes | Swiss Cottage |
| Miss Rose Goodwin | Grocer |
| Bick Brothers | Nursery |
| John Bradley | Jobbing Bricklayer |
| Fred Andrews | Greengrocer |
| and  R Haviland | Cycle Agent |

Mr Evans the Fruiterer also sold fish, rabbits and vegetables. There was a large field behind his shop, in which he kept the horse used for deliveries. Shopping in those days was not the hustle and bustle business that it is today, for many of the traders mentioned spent a lot of time calling for, and delivering orders, as Mr Chubb's advertisement shows.

Bishops, the Drapers, was run by Mr and Mrs Bishop and their daughter Mildred, and they sold material by the yard, sheets, blankets and underwear. They also stocked clothes which could be tried on behind a curtained partition.

Frank Biddle the Chemist was a well-known and much loved figure in Olton, as well as at the Congregational Church where he was a Deacon. (Plate 48) His shop window contained blue and green Apothecaries bottles to advertise his trade. Inside the shop there were beautiful little mahogany drawers with Latin labels, in which he kept his powders and potions.

Plate 48                                                          Frank Biddle.

Mr Biddle had qualified as a Registered Chemist and Druggist on the 2nd January 1895, and opened his business in Olton during 1906. Working Class Oltonians, who could not afford to pay the bills of local doctors Cox and Lunn, often consulted Mr Biddle who had a particularly successful rheumatism medicine, and also a very good cough remedy. He was specially interested in skin troubles too, and people came to him from all over the city for advice on such complaints. He made up prescriptions in a small hallway behind the shop, and his own children were never allowed into the chemists in case they embarrassed customers who were describing their ailments.

Mr Biddle was a very keen amateur photographer, and many of his local scenes were made up into Post-cards which he sold in the shop. Examples of his excellent photography in Olton can be seen on Plate 16, 18 and 37. All Frank Biddle's Post-cards pre-date the First World War, during which his son John was killed. Both had shared a common love of photography, and Mr Biddle's interest in the subject died with his son. Harold Allman also sold Post-cards at the Post Office and News-agents that he ran.

To the Northern end of the shops were a group of four cottages and two houses, one of which was occupied by Sergeant Lawrence the friendly local policeman. He walked his beat, or rode on his bicycle, and was vigilant in checking that all the shops were securely locked up at night. If the locals drank too much down the alleyway by Mushams wine shop, Sergeant Lawrence would escort them home briskly, but he did not charge them.

Traders children often played in the field behind Mr Evans shop, and if they strayed onto the railway embankment Sergeant Lawrence would beat them, with his rolled up police cape. He never really hurt them though. Sergeant Lawrence was not the only policeman in Olton, for several others were stationed in the house, which is now an Old Peoples Home, called "Olton Grange". This was the Police Station on the Warwick Road, near "Olton Hollow" for many years.

There was also a sub-Fire Station, a small wooden building contain-ing a manual Fire engine on the Old Warwick Road, near its Northerly junction with the Warwick Road. The shops were all set well back from the road behind a wide pavement adorned with hawthorn trees, which were particularly beautiful when they flowered in Spring-time.

Olton's aesthetic heritage has, until now, gone largely unheralded. Yet within the confines of St Bernard's Road, Kineton Green Road and parts of the Warwick Road, there is undoubtedly a fine collection of domestic stained glass. Many Victorian vestibule doors in St Bernard's Road contain stained glass windows, enriched with a wide variety of delicately painted natural subjects, which include birds, flowers and leaves.

In the 1870's there were at least seventeen stained glass firms in the Birmingham area, but the available documentation of their work, for domestic purposes, is almost non-existent. Well known businesses such as Hardman's, Osler's and Winfield's are probably responsible for at least some of the many fine examples to be found in the Olton Conservation Area.

The Hardman Archives in Birmingham Library give details of work done at "The Lodge", Berry Hall, Solihull in 1884, enriched with paintings of birds, the description of which bears a strong resemblance to several domestic stained glass doors in St Bernard's Road. The firm claims responsibility for some domestic stained glass work in Olton, and also executed the West front window in St Margaret's Church, dedicated to the men who were lost in the Great War.

The variety of Victorian stained glass and hand-painted domestic windows in Olton are complemented by the numerous contrasting Edwardian designs for windows in the area, which rely totally on the colour and shape of the glass and lead for effect. There is no evidence in Olton of additional painting on secular stained glass during and after this period. Floral themes in rich colours abound, and the diversity of design in windows within a comparatively small area is amazing. The tulip shape was obviously popular, to be succeeded in about 1914 by stylized roses. At least three houses in Kineton Green Road and St Bernard's Road have windows depicting complete landscapes, with hills, fields, trees and birds. These scenes date from around 1911, and the example illustrated is from St. Bernard's Road. (Plate 48)

The influence of the Arts and Craft Movement is evident in several houses in the Olton Conservation Area. (Plate 49) Perhaps the best individual example is "The Spinney", No. 74 St Bernard's Road. Local architect, Harry Bloomer designed it, and the strong roof lines of this building, with its sweeping gables give it much of its character. Similar features are evident at "Barton", now No. 45 Kineton Green Road which Mr Bloomer designed for his own occupation. The adjacent semi-detached house "Afton", No. 43, is a mirror image of "Barton". All

Plate 49

Domestic stained glass window in St. Bernard's Road.

three aforementioned houses were built around 1911, and it is known that Geoff Mobbs built "The Spinney" which shows the influence of Charles F. Annesley Voysey in its design. Harry Bloomer's later work dated from around 1914 can also be seen in Number 47 — 53 Kineton Green Road.

Internal features at "The Spinney" include a superb goache frieze of scenes from Robin Hood, painted on the wall above the picture rail, around the complete circumference of an oak panelled room. The artists were Nora Yoxall and Elsie Whitford, who were students of Miss Hall at the Birmingham Art School in the late 1920s. The house also has superb door furniture in brass and copper, some of which is embellished with Ruskin pottery.

"Briar Cottage", Number 103 St Bernard's Road is another example of domestic architecture influenced by the Arts and Craft Movement. Its architect was W.J. Davis, a Birmingham man, who also designed the house next door but one (Number 107). "Briar Cottage" was built for Oliver Middleton, circa 1908, and remained in the ownership of his family until 1982 when his daughter Olwen died. Probably because of this many original features, including lamp fittings, have remained to this day.

The contrast between buildings such as "The Spinney", "Briar Cottage", and the much larger, but equally beautiful Victorian and Edwardian houses is part of the charm of the Olton Conservation Area, and is most evident in Kineton Green Road which is a complete mixture of styles and periods.

*Olton Artists*

Late 19th and early 20th Century Olton, with its peaceful rural settings, (Plate 50) naturally had a magnetic effect on artists, and people with a strong aesthetic appreciation. Husband and wife team Georgie and Arthur Gaskin, whose influence was very evident in the Birmingham Arts and Craft Movement, are known to have been in Olton in 1895, and were living at Number 32 (then 16) St Bernard's Road between 1911 and 1918, as tenants of Edward Meredith Evans. Both husband and wife are famous for their book illustrations, metalwork, and especially as jewellery designers and crafters. From 1903 until 1924 Arthur Gaskin was Head of the School of Jewellers and Silversmiths in Vittoria Street, Birmingham.

Plate 50

An Edwardian lady beside Boundary Brook (Kineton Brook) in early spring.

Georgie was evidently a leader of fashion, and is depicted with one of her two daughters in the foreground of a painting by Joseph Southall entitled "Corporation Street, Birmingham in 1914", at the top of the main staircase in Birmingham Museum and Art Gallery. This museum, and the Victoria and Albert Museum in London, have many examples of the Gaskin's work (particularly their jewellery) which is periodically displayed. Cheltenham Museum also has some examples of the Gaskin's jewellery.

William T. Blackband, the Gaskin's friend and Arthur's successor as Head of the School of Jewellers and Silversmiths, also made his home in Olton, on the Warwick Road. He is buried in the Cemetery of Olton Friary. Like the Gaskins, examples of his work can be seen in Birmingham Museum.

The poet, John Drinkwater, during a stay at the Gaskin's St Bernard's Road home, with its beautiful views over Olton Reservoir, wrote a poem about this expanse of water in his collection of poems entitled "Olton Pools". It is an evocative poem that paints a picture of the Reservoir in early summer.

No book on Olton would be complete without mention of its most widely known artist Edith Holden, who is famous for her best-selling "Nature Notes of 1906" written in Olton, and published in 1977 as "The Country Diary of an Edwardian Lady".

Arthur Holden, with three of his daughters, Winifred, Violet and Edith, moved into "Gowan Bank" (Number 15 Kineton Green Road) in 1905. They became the tenants of James Thomas Grice, who had bought roughly 2 acres of land bridging St Bernard's Road and Kineton Green Road from John Collingwood Onions in 1896. Eight houses were built on this land, which was subject to the £500 minimum building cost covenant, laid down by the Executors of the late William Williams Estate, as mentioned by Margaret Jordan in Chapter 6 page 50.

Thus the Holdens moved into a brand new and extremely well built house completed early in 1905 by Bragg the builders. Mr Grice's son-in-law, George Jackson Blunn, moved into "The Whins" (Number 19) next door but one, in 1912, just before the Holdens left, after Edith's marriage to the sculptor Ernest Smith.

As it was rented, the Holden name does not appear on the deeds of Number 15 Kineton Green Road, but the words "Gowan Bank" do. The family called three of their several homes by this name, which obviously meant a lot to them, "Gowan" being the Scottish word for "daisy".

In the Biography of Edith Holden by Ina Taylor entitled "The Edwardian Lady", we are told that Arthur Holden was a Unitarian. However, he and one of his daughters, (the records do not reveal which) also rented a pew at the Congregational Church opposite "Gowan Bank". Edith, like her deceased Mother before her, was drawn to Spiritualism, Josephine Poole informs us in "The Country Diary Companion".

Word of the sceances held at "Gowan Bank" in the early Twentieth Century, soon spread along Kineton Green Road and John Jessop's two youngest daughters Muriel and Frances, (seen in Plate 44) always scuttled past the house for fear of unseen spirits, on their way to Miss Allinghams school at the corner of the road. The sceances ceased at the house when the Holdens left, but the desire to write lives on. Two more books written by separate residents in the sixties and seventies at "Gowan Bank", were published a year before Edith Holden's Diary appeared in print, in 1977. Over seventy years separated the writing of the three books, yet they were all published within twelve months of each other. Now exactly eighty years after Edith Holden compiled her Nature Notes, this book on the story of Olton's history has been published. Changing Scenes and Famous People was compiled at "Gowan Bank".

# BIBLIOGRAPHY

| | |
|---|---|
| Geographica | Strabo |
| The Conquest of Gaul | Caesar |
| The History of the Kings of Britain | Geoffrey of Monmouth |
| Florence of Worcester in 'Church Historians of England'. | J. Stevenson |
| The Anglo-Saxon Chronicles | (Everyman editions) |
| Alfred the Great | trans. Keynes & Lapidge |
| Anglo-Saxon England | Stenton |
| Geology-in 'The Coventry District Naturalists Guide' | F.W. Shotton MBE., FRS |
| Encylopaedia Britannica | |
| A History of the English Church and its people | Bede |
| Domesday Book—Warwickshire (History from the sources) | Plaiter Morris |
| Domesday Geography of the Midlands | Darby |
| A Dictionary of British Surnames | Reaney |
| Domesday Book to Magna Carta | Poole |
| Life of Anselm | Eadmer |
| English Monasteries | Dugdale |
| Warwick Castle & its Earls Vol.1. | Frances Countess of Warwick |
| Ingulphus Abbot of Croyland in 'Church Historians of England' | J. Stevenson |
| The History of the County of Hampshire | Victoria County History |
| The Thirteenth Century | Powicke |
| The Antiquities of Warwickshire | Dugdale |
| Baronacy | Dugdale |
| The Red Book of the Exchequer | Edited—Hearne |
| Calendars of Close Rolls | Birm. ref. library |
| Calendars of Charter Rolls | Birm. ref. library |
| The Historical Antiquities of Hertfordshire | Chauncy |
| English History | Matthew Paris trans. Giles |
| The History of the County of Hertfordshire | Victoria County History |
| The History of the County of Warwickshire | Victoria County History |
| Memorials of the Family of Wilson (compiled in 1927) | Warwick records office |
| Solihull and its School | Burman |

| Caroline Clive — from the Diary and family papers | Edited—Mary Clive |
| An History of Birmingham | Hutton |
| Solihull and its Church | Pemberton |
| Josiah Mason Trust Archives | |
| Olton United Reformed Church Archives | |
| Olton College for Girls (Bickenhill Hall) | Prospectus 1899 |
| The Dream Palaces of Birmingham | Chris & Rosemary Clegg |
| The Hardman Archives | Birm. ref. library |
| Arthur & Georgie Gaskin | Catalogue of 1982 exhibition Birmingham museum & art gallery |
| | |
| Olton Pools | John Drinkwater |
| The Edwardian Lady | Ina Taylor |
| The Country Diary of an Edwardian Lady | Edith Holden |
| The Country Diary Companion | Josephine Poole |
| Warwickshire Cricketers | Santall |
| Kelly's Directories — 1880-1920 | |
| Census Returns — 1841–1881 | |
| The Origins of Solihull | Victor Skipp |
| Discovering Bickenhill | Victor Skipp |
| The old roads of England | Sir William Addison |
| Canals of the West Midlands | Charles Hadfield |
| 1000 years of Yardley — A History of the Birmingham/Warwick Canal & a survey of the Railways | |
| From cabin boy to Archbishop. The Autobiography of Bishop Ullathorne | From original draft with intro. by Leslie Shane |
| St Margaret's — The first 100 years | Robert Kay |
| The life of an Engineer | Dr P.W. Kinsford |
| The Steel Pen Trade | A.A.S. Charles |
| The Book of Household Management | Isabella Beeton |
| The Rise and Fall of the Victorian Servant | Pamela Horn |
| Life below stairs | Frank Huggett |
| Census and Social Structure | Edited by Richard Lawton |
| The Victorian Countryside | Edited by G.E. Mingay |
| Olton Conservation | Prepared by Residents study group — Olton |

# INDEX